THE LITERATURE
Review

3
EDITION

THE LITERATURE
Review SIX STEPS TO SUCCESS

3
EDITION

Lawrence A. Machi

Brenda T. McEvoy

CORWIN
A SAGE Publishing Company

FOR INFORMATION:

Corwin

A SAGE Company

2455 Teller Road

Thousand Oaks, California 91320

(800) 233-9936

www.corwin.com

SAGE Publications Ltd.

1 Oliver's Yard

55 City Road

London EC1Y 1SP

United Kingdom

SAGE Publications India Pvt. Ltd.

B 1/I 1 Mohan Cooperative Industrial Area

Mathura Road, New Delhi 110 044

India

SAGE Publications Asia-Pacific Pte. Ltd.

3 Church Street

#10-04 Samsung Hub

Singapore 049483

Senior Acquisitions Editor: Arnis Burvikovs

Associate Editor: Desirée A. Bartlett

Senior Editorial Assistant: Andrew Olson

Production Editor: Veronica Stapleton Hooper

Copy Editor: Shannon Kelly

Typesetter: C&M Digitals (P) Ltd.

Proofreader: Dennis W. Webb

Indexer: Molly Hall

Cover Designer: Candice Harman

Marketing Manager: Anna Mesick

Library of Congress Cataloging-in-Publication Data

Names: Machi, Lawrence A. | McEvoy, Brenda T.

Title: The literature review : six steps to success / Lawrence A. Machi, Brenda T. McEvoy.

Description: Third edition. | Thousand Oaks, California: Corwin, [2016] | Includes bibliographical references and index.

Identifiers: LCCN 2015048510 | ISBN 9781506336244 (pbk. : alk. paper)

Subjects: LCSH: Research—Methodology—Study and teaching (Secondary)—Handbooks, manuals, etc. | Research—Methodology—Study and teaching (Higher)—Handbooks, manuals, etc. | Research—Methodology—Handbooks, manuals, etc.

Classification: LCC LB1047.3.M33 2016 | DDC 001.4—dc23 LC record available at http://lccn.loc.gov/2015048510

This book is printed on acid-free paper.

Certified Chain of Custody
Promoting Sustainable Forestry
www.sfiprogram.org
SFI-01268

SFI label applies to text stock

18 19 20 21 22 10 9 8 7 6 5

Contents

Literature Review Flowchart

Step 4. Survey the Literature

📖 **Task 1.** Assemble the Collected Data
  - ○ *Activity 1. Catalog the Data*

📖 **Task 2.** Organize the Information
  - ○ *Activity 1. Arrange Information to Build Evidence*
  - ○ *Activity 2. Organize the Information and Build Claims*

📖 **Task 3.** Analyze the Patterns of Data
  - ○ *Activity 1. Map the Discovery Argument*
  - ○ *Activity 2. Analyze the Argument*

Step 5. Critique the Literature

📖 **Concept 1.** Making the Case for the Literature Review

📖 **Concept 2.** Descriptive Argument Patterns: Factual Reasoning

📖 **Concept 3.** Implicative Argument Patterns: Implicative Reasoning

📖 **Concept 4.** The Implicative Argument: Nine Basic Patterns

📖 **Concept 5.** Backing

📖 Doing a Critique of the Literature

📖 **Task 1.** Determine Logic Pattern Inferred by Study Topic

📖 **Task 2.** Reframe Claims to Meet Conditions Required by Logic Type

📖 **Task 3.** Build the Advocacy Argument

📖 **Concept 6.** Fallacies

📖 **Concept 7.** The Case Is Everything

Step 6. Write the Review

📖 **Task 1.** Write to Understand
  - ○ *Activity 1. Review Notes and Memoranda*
  - ○ *Activity 2. Exploratory Write*
  - ○ *Activity 3. Outline*
  - ○ *Activity 4. Write Preliminary Draft*

📖 **Task 2.** Write to Be Understood
  - ○ *Activity 1. Write the First Draft*
  - ○ *Activity 2. Revise—Working the Second and Third Drafts*
  - ○ *Activity 3. Complete the Final Draft*

✓ **Submit the Literature Review**

Preface

Creating a successful literature review is a complex project. This book serves as a logical road map to guide the researcher from finding a topic to researching, organizing, arguing, and composing the review. The many and varied skills needed for this project are sure to be more difficult to employ if learning is confined to trial and error. Here, gathered into one volume, are many of the strategies, tools, and techniques used by experienced researchers intent on building a high-quality literature review.

NEW TO THIS EDITION

This third edition has been updated, expanded, and newly reorganized to improve ease of use.

- The six-step process is directly aligned and explained using an applied critical-thinking model that demonstrates the logical progression needed to produce a quality literature review, while taking the mystery out of the process.
- Additional online guides and guidance have been added.
- *Reflective Oversight* boxes have been added to each chapter to direct metacognitive activities.
- New and updated graphics are included.
- Additional key vocabulary words have been added to the beginning of chapters and to the glossary.
- The process has been further simplified through topical reorganization and by the addition of lists of concepts that introduce Chapters 2–6. These lists make it easier for the reader to quickly find a needed concept.
- Examples have been expanded and added.
- More explanations and tips are provided for writing in the early stages of the project.

AUDIENCE

- Students wishing to preview the completion of a required literature review will find this book helpful as a means of clarifying what will be expected.
- Beginning researchers will find the book an excellent tool for learning the craft of producing a successful research project.

- More advanced students may use this text to review their skills and perhaps discover a few new tips.
- Those teaching the craft of research will find here an excellent class text for their students.

This book is mainly intended for two groups of researchers: those completing master's theses and those working on doctoral dissertations. For those doing a class research assignment or completing most master's degree projects, the text will address the type of literature review that summarizes and evaluates the existing knowledge on a particular topic. Some master's theses, and all doctoral dissertations, require a more sophisticated literature review. This book is also useful for the initial stage of completing a complex literature review, one that requires the student to argue and define a problem needing original research.

While much of the book uses education as its context, the model, strategies, and tools presented apply to a much wider audience within the social sciences. Because education is an applied science, many of the examples and strategies contained in this book consider the literature from a variety of vantage points, including social and organizational psychology, sociology, and group psychology. Thus, students studying these disciplines will also find this text helpful.

SPECIAL FEATURES AND TEXT ORGANIZATION

All students, beginning or advanced, can profit from a straightforward guide for maneuvering through the ambiguities of framing the topic, finding and managing information, developing the argument, and acquiring the composition skills needed to produce a successful literature review. There are definite tricks of the trade for making this project an efficient and rewarding experience. This text is organized using an applied critical-thinking model. The six-step literature review process guides the reader logically through the project. These steps are as follows:

- Step 1. Select a topic.
- Step 2. Develop the argument.
- Step 3. Search the literature.
- Step 4. Survey the literature.
- Step 5. Critique the literature.
- Step 6. Write the review.

Each chapter addresses a specific step of this model and contains several learning aids to increase reader comprehension. These learning aids include the following:

- Key vocabulary terms appear at the beginning of each chapter, allowing the reader to focus on key ideas.
- A chapter overview outlines the content of each chapter as a readiness tool.
- Exercises assist the reader through the more involved procedures. These guided practice opportunities and examples aid in making sure the reader understands the text.
- Specific references suggest software that can simplify the work of organizing material and revising the written composition.
- Graphics and charts clarify the key topics under discussion, and models present pictures that tie together complex themes and procedures.
- At the end of each chapter, tips provide specific ideas for using the material covered in the chapter. These tips help the reader make immediate, practical use of the material.
- Each chapter has a summary that gives a brief recap of the chapter's contents and acts as an aid for the reader to review information.
- Each chapter also contains a checklist. These lists allow the reader to track progress through the entire literature review project.
- The chapters end with reflective oversight boxes, which direct the reader to metacognition activities related to the chapter content.
- The end of the text contains a glossary of definitions of frequently used terms and a reference list of works for further reading.

When confronting the task of successfully producing a literature review, there are three choices. The researcher can proceed in an organized fashion using a book such as this one as a guide. It is also possible to search the Internet or go to YouTube and play roulette with a myriad of entries and explanations, hoping to find legitimate guidance. Or one can plunge blindly into the project and try to find the time and resources needed while hoping for the best. Experienced researchers know that trial and error is frustrating, time consuming, and rarely successful. Learning the key ideas in this text will promote success while limiting frustration and lost time.

Acknowledgments

Corwin gratefully acknowledges the contributions of the following reviewers:

Andrea M. Capizzi
Assistant Professor of the Practice of Special Education
Vanderbilt University
Nashville, Tennessee

Lori Helman
Associate Professor of Literacy Education
University of Minnesota, Twin Cities
Minneapolis, Minnesota

Maureen K. Lienau
Professor of Education and Chair of Cognitive Studies
Ashford University
Denver, Colorado

About the Authors

Lawrence A. Machi is a professor emeritus of organizational leadership at the University of La Verne, in La Verne, California. He holds an MA in curriculum development and an Ed.D. in organizational leadership. He has taught research methods and design and has chaired doctoral dissertation research in addition to teaching classes in organizational development. He has extensive experience in higher education, and prior to his tenure at La Verne, he taught in schools of education at the University of San Francisco, St. Mary's College of California, and Sonoma State University. Dr. Machi currently serves as a Fulbright Specialist and recently completed an assignment in Taiwan.

With K–12 experience as well, he has worked as a secondary teacher and served as a school administrator in both secondary and elementary school districts in northern California. He has occupied the roles of vice principal, principal, assistant superintendent, and superintendent, frequently consulting with many California school districts and nonprofit organizations. His specialties are in the areas of organizational leadership, finance, negotiations, organizational development, and strategic thinking.

Brenda T. McEvoy taught high school English, history, and science for 36 years. Research skills were always part of her curriculum. For 8 years, she worked for the California State Department of Education, leading groups of educators in improving their ability to edit and assess student writing. She was also a mentor for beginning English and history teachers in California. Participation in the California Writing Project extended her knowledge of writing and the difficulties students face when producing a major assignment. She has worked as an editor for several books, focusing on helping writers create work that is clear and logical.

Introduction

Doing and Producing a Literature Review

An Overview

GETTING STARTED

Chi ha fretta vada piano.

In order to go fast, you must go slow.

KEY VOCABULARY

- **Complex Literature Review**—A review that extends the work of the simple review to identify and define an unanswered question requiring new primary research.

- **Literature Review**—A written document that develops a case to establish a thesis. This case is based on a comprehensive understanding of the current knowledge of the topic. A literature review synthesizes current knowledge pertaining to the research question. This synthesis is the foundation that, through the use of logical argumentation, allows the researcher to build a convincing thesis case.

- **Reflective Oversight**—A contemplative thought process that critically regulates, assesses, and corrects the personal knowledge, skills, and tasks used to conduct the literature review.

(Continued)

1

(Continued)

- **Simple Literature Review**—A written document that critically reviews the relevant literature on a research topic, presenting a logical case that establishes a thesis delineating what is currently known about the subject.

- **Thesis Statement**—A declarative sentence that expresses a conclusion based on a case developed using existing knowledge, sound evidence, and reasoned argument.

- **Topic**—A research area refined by interest, an academic discipline, and an understanding of relevant key works and core concepts.

So you need to produce a literature review. Perhaps this is a class assignment, a thesis for a master's degree, or the foundation research for a doctoral dissertation. Whether approaching this task for the first time or as an experienced researcher, we all do it for the same reasons: to increase our skills and knowledge, to learn, to share, and also to have the satisfaction of completing a successful project. To succeed, you will want to avoid the problem mentioned by a colleague of the authors: "Some people do not have the patience and foresight to do it right the first time, but have infinite patience and capacity to do it over, and over, and over again."

The good news is that you do not need to reinvent the literature review process. Trial and error isn't the only approach. There are known procedures and skills to make this task easier and more efficient. This book provides a road map to guide you in producing a literature review that will contribute to your field. Conscientiously using this book will help you arrive successfully at your destination. Each chapter offers tips and tools from many sources, including ones from the authors' experience. Using the six-step process offered here will make it possible to plan and complete a successful literature review without wasting time and effort.

CHAPTER OVERVIEW

This introductory chapter presents the key concepts to be mastered to produce a quality literature review. They are procedure, disposition, and reflection. The chapter begins by defining the purpose and procedure for doing a literature review. Simply knowing correct procedure will not guarantee success, however. How you are disposed to engage in this endeavor and to self-evaluate the quality and accuracy of the work will weigh heavily on your success. This chapter presents the personal dispositions necessary to complete a project of this scope and the reflection process used to manage and evaluate the quality and accuracy of the work.

THE PURPOSE OF A LITERATURE REVIEW

As you begin, ask yourself, "Am I trying to present a position, *a thesis*, that defines the current state of knowledge about a topic, or am I using the current knowledge about a topic as the basis for arguing a thesis that defines a research problem for further study?"

Literature reviews have different purposes depending on the nature of the inquiry. If the purpose of the inquiry is to argue a position about the current state of knowledge on a topic, then you are doing a **simple literature review**. If the purpose of the inquiry is to review the literature to uncover a research problem for further study, then you are doing a **complex literature review**.

The simple literature review (Figure I.1) documents, analyzes, and draws conclusions about what is known about a particular topic. Its purpose is to produce a position on the state of that knowledge; this is the **thesis statement**.

Figure I.1   The Simple Literature Review

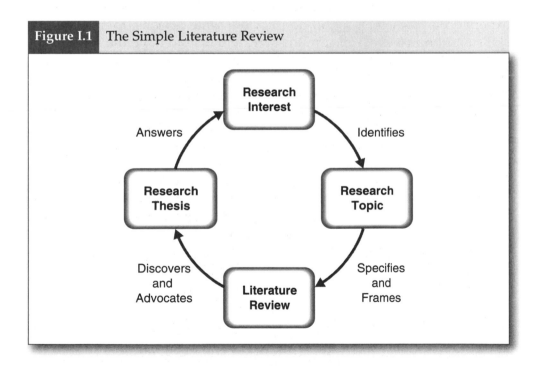

The simple literature review begins by selecting and identifying a research interest for inquiry. This is the preliminary study question. As you proceed, you will narrow and refine this interest into a research topic, based on an initial exploration of the literature. The research topic must be a clear and concise statement that defines and describes what will be researched. Its definition identifies and frames the scope of the literature review. The literature review canvasses the literature, documenting and cataloging pertinent knowledge. From this information, it presents an evidence-based analysis of the present understanding of the topic. The product of the simple literature review is the development of a case that argues what is known about the topic. The case's conclusion is a thesis statement that answers the question posed by the research interest. Many class research assignments and master's degree thesis projects require a simple literature review.

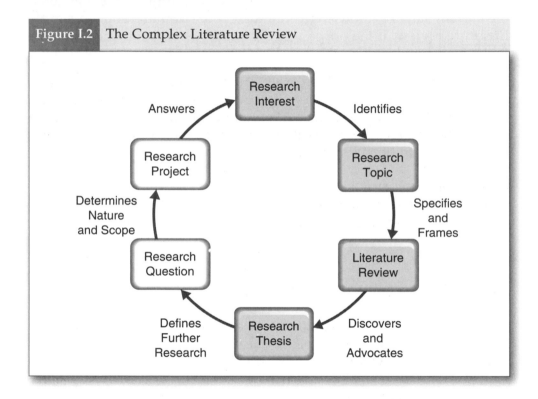

Figure I.2   The Complex Literature Review

The complex literature review (Figure I.2) has a different purpose and additional demands. It not only presents the current state of knowledge about a topic (the darkened four boxes of Figure I.2) but must also argue how this knowledge reasonably leads to a problem or to a question requiring original research.

In the complex literature review, the researcher first addresses the current state of knowledge about the study question. Then, based on these findings, the researcher proposes a thesis defining an issue for further study. This thesis becomes the problem or question of a new research study. The conclusions drawn not only define the research question but also frame the appropriate methods to be used for conducting the research.

Advanced master's theses and doctoral dissertations use the complex literature review as the basis for providing the background statements and the argument for the research study. The complex literature review is used to write Chapter 1 (Introduction) and Chapter 2 (Review of the Literature) of the standard five-chapter dissertation document. Not having a quality literature review in hand when developing these chapters will surely result in numerous unsuccessful attempts. "You can't write about what you don't know," as the saying goes. The complex literature review is the starting point for research projects such as dissertations.

While simple reviews and complex reviews seek different outcomes, the manner in which they uncover knowledge and produce a thesis is similar.

THE LITERATURE REVIEW DEFINED

A **literature review** is a written argument that supports a thesis position by building a case from credible evidence obtained from previous research. It provides the context and the background about the current knowledge of the topic and lays out a logical case to defend the conclusions it draws. Here is our definition of a literature review:

> *A literature review is a written document that presents a logically argued case founded on a comprehensive understanding of the current state of knowledge about a topic of study. This case establishes a convincing thesis to answer the study's question.*

THE LITERATURE REVIEW PROCESS

A literature review is an organized way to research a chosen topic. Let's take the mystery out of this process. The simple fact is that doing a literature review is an exercise in applied critical thinking.

Critically thinking about an issue is a deliberate process. First, the subject of the inquiry must be recognized. It must be clearly defined and described. Once a researcher has a clear definition of the subject in question, information can now be collected about the topic. These **data** are cataloged and organized in such a fashion that some sense can be made of them. The data can then be interpreted and analyzed to build the evidence or reasons to form conclusions. The conclusions formed present the logical case for answering the question first inquired about. Finally, the argument is examined; the researcher looks for holes in the reasoning and weighs the conclusions drawn against competing alternatives. Once this process is completed, the answer can be shared with others.

Figure I.3 shows the steps for conducting a literature review, as matched to the applied critical-thinking process.

As is critical thinking, doing a literature review is a developmental process in which each step leads to the next (Figure I.3). Following is a brief explanation of these six steps.

Figure I.3   The Literature Review Is a Critical-Thinking Process

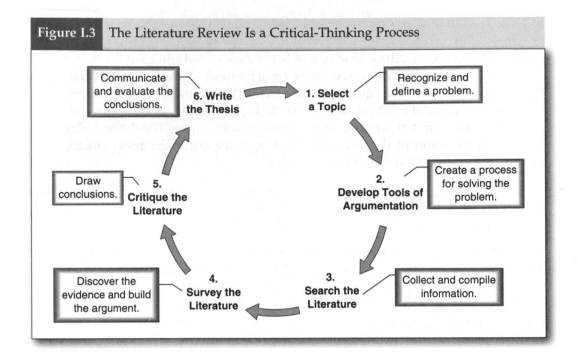

Step 1. Select a Topic—*Recognize and Define the Problem*

A successful research topic is usually the offspring of an interest in a practical problem. The interest statement must be reshaped appropriately, converting its generic wording to specific academic language. The topic statement must be well defined to allow the researcher to successfully identify the appropriate literature in the pertinent academic discipline. Refining the terms used, accurately framing the focus of the interest, and selecting the appropriate academic knowledge base are the tasks to be completed to define a research topic.

Step 1. Select the Topic is also the start of the writing process. Keeping a written journal of your progress begins here and is essential to comprehending and building knowledge. A journal helps to clarify ideas and process learning. Writing helps clarify thoughts and ideas. The journal is an ideal place to establish an internal dialogue where reflection on your learning can be "wrestled with" and understood. Journals also provide an excellent place for planning and reviewing work.

Step 2. Develop the Tools for Argument—*Create a Process for Solving the Problem*

Since a literature review must present a logically argued case founded on a comprehensive understanding of the current state of knowledge, then the rules and tools for building an informal argument must be employed. A credible case is not simply reporting about a collection of information or presenting your opinion about the topic. A credible case produces conclusions resulting from a logical presentation of supporting evidence. The tools for evidence building, argument development, and logical reasoning are the building blocks used to make a credible case.

A literature review uses two types of argument to build its case. The first argument builds the findings of the case. The second argument forms the case's conclusions. The result is a well-argued thesis. Both arguments are based on sound reasoning and logical construction. The knowledge and the application of the processes and tools of argumentation are the means for constructing a literature review.

Step 3. Search the Literature—*Collect and Organize the Information*

A literature search determines the data to be included in the review. It does this by winnowing the research information to only the data that provide the strongest evidence to support the thesis case. When searching the literature, preview, select, and organize the data for study by using the skills of skimming, scanning, and mapping the data. Next, the researcher catalogs and documents the relevant data.

Step 4. Survey the Literature—*Discover the Evidence and Build Findings*

The literature survey assembles, organizes, and analyzes the data on the current knowledge about the topic. The data are logically arranged as evidence to produce a set of defensible findings about what is known concerning the topic.

Step 5. Critique the Literature—*Draw Conclusions*

The literature critique interprets the findings produced by the survey of literature. The findings are logically arranged as conclusions to form the argument that justifies the thesis statement. The critique analyzes how current knowledge answers the research question.

Step 6. Write the Review—*Communicate and Evaluate the Conclusions*

Writing the review produces a document that communicates the results of the project. Through a process of composing and refining, the literature review document becomes a work that accurately conveys to an intended audience the results of the research. This composition requires writing, auditing, and editing to produce a polished final product—one that is accurate, complete, and understandable. Writing done in the first five steps of the literature review is used as the foundation for writing the review.

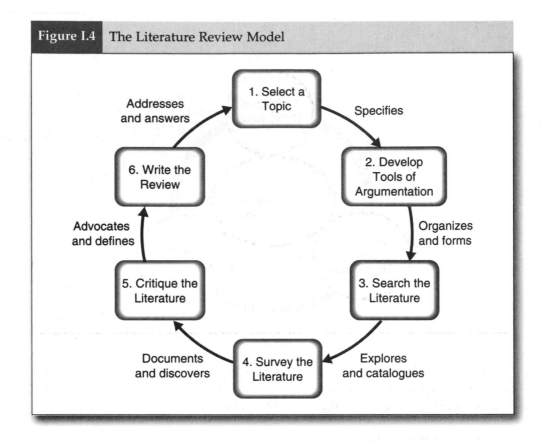

| Figure I.4 | The Literature Review Model |

The above discussion, although condensed, relates the procedural steps necessary to complete a literature review. The following chapters will fully describe each step and will provide help to complete each of the tasks necessary for building a strong thesis case and conducting a good review.

We turn now to examining the mental attitude and stance necessary to complete a project. The next two sections of this chapter will discuss the personal dispositions required to take on this task and the reflection process used to manage and evaluate the quality and accuracy of the work.

MINDSET: PERSONAL DISPOSITIONS ON THINKING, DOING, AND DECIDING

A person's mental and emotional state plays a vital role in the outcome of the work undertaken. If this state is negative, a successful outcome is doubtful. As discussed earlier in this chapter, the procedure for doing a literature review is an application of a critical-thinking process. Critical thinking, however, is not just a recipe for thinking, it is also a specific mindset—a particular mental and emotional state. This mindset or disposition defines how you choose to be and to act when working on an analytical task such as a literature review.

Figure I.5	The Inquirer's Mindset

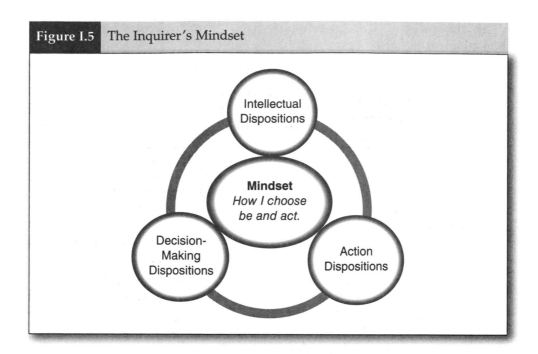

As depicted in Figure I.5, the critical thinker's mindset can be divided into three types of dispositions: intellect, action, and decision making. Each disposition identifies its traits and behaviors.

Intellectual Dispositions

Intellectual dispositions describe the type of thinking a person chooses to use when engaging in a task. A critical thinker chooses to be:

- *Inquisitive.* All successful critical thinking begins with curiosity. To think critically, one must have an inquiring mind, a natural curiosity, and a fundamental need to learn and to discover. Curiosity creates the sparks that ignite a need to explore what lies beyond the currently known. This fire, in turn, sprouts the seeds that become the fragile beginnings of the research itself. Critical thinkers continually approach their work with questions such as "Why?" "What if?" and "Is it true?" These questions and others like them stimulate the inquiry and fuel the critical-thinking process.

- *Skeptical.* The critical thinker is constantly raising questions. This thinker advances with skepticism and questions everything. What is being said? What does it mean? Is it supported by good evidence? Are the conclusions reasonably and logically drawn? An inquirer is constantly learning, reflecting on past work in order to navigate the present work. This thinker maintains a healthy disregard for accepted positions and questions the factual and logical basis for any conclusions. The critical thinker knows that everyone has biases, opinions, beliefs, values, and experiences that create a unique perspective and attempts to keep these in perspective.

- *Independent.* Critical thinkers do not blindly accept the positions and conclusions of others but think for themselves. They are in the habit of raising questions, finding the relevant information, building reasoned positions, and developing their own conclusions. They seek and set standards for clarity of thought, relevance of information, and reasonableness for the positions they take. Critical thinkers are not satisfied until they truly understand both the issue under consideration and a reasonable response that addresses it.

- *Honest.* Critical thinkers hold themselves accountable for their biases, viewpoints, and the conclusions taken. They continually examine and reflect on the veracity of their positions, weighing them against new facts and ideas. They suspend judgment until all facts have been gathered and considered. They can adjust and reject their opinions and positions when new facts become known.

Action Dispositions

Action dispositions describe the behaviors and traits exhibited by a critical thinker engaged in a task. Critical thinkers exercise:

- *Persistence.* The critical thinker is diligent. Regardless of the number of hours of painstaking work, the confusion and miscues encountered, or the tedium and magnitude of the task, they stay with a project until it is completed. They are dogged about seeking relevant information, following all leads and exhausting all possibilities.

- *Patience.* Critical thinkers take the time necessary to carefully and thoroughly complete the work before them. They calmly and deliberately work through the task. They strive to be precise and understand that context and subject matter dictate precision.

- *Deliberation.* Critical thinkers take care to focus on the concern at hand. They strive to maintain orderliness when working with complex tasks. They recognize their own limitations and strive to correct their discrepancies. Critical thinkers look for the nuances when reviewing information, constantly searching for connections and patterns in the data. They take care to see both the trees and the forest.

- *Collegiality.* Critical thinkers are able to share ideas and conclusions with others for feedback and evaluation. They seek out the criticism of others with the knowledge that sharing their information confirms or improves it.

Decision-Making Dispositions

Decision-making dispositions are the thought processes used when solving problems and deciding the directions to pursue when engaging in a task. They are:

- *Reasoned and logical thinking.* Critical thinkers prefer to employ rational thinking and weigh all data for their veracity and value. They seek evidence, examine the pros and cons of any question, and take positions based on strong evidence. Critical thinkers trust in the process of reasoned thinking, evidence building, and rational arguments to make their decisions.

- *Circumspect thinking.* Critical thinkers approach the research with an open mind, considering and learning from divergent viewpoints. They strive to maintain objectivity and guard against having any predetermined conclusions. The critical thinker is open to seeing all results of an inquiry and weighing the value of each piece of evidence and each position taken. When taking a position, this thinker maintains flexibility in considering alternatives. The critical thinker reflects continually.

ETHICS

No discussion about mindset would be complete without addressing the moral issue of ethical behavior.

Every undertaking has a code of ethics. Researching and writing are no different. Consider the following tenants before you begin work:

- Do not take data out of context. Researchers may not manipulate data to defend a preferred outcome. This is not just a matter of fabricating data. It also includes extending their value.
- Do your own research. Librarians and other assistants are there to point you in the right direction, but they should not be the ones to paddle the canoe through the research sites and library stacks. Doing your own research is especially important when researching online where information is available without regard to its veracity.
- Present only what you believe to be factual. Do not use fallacious arguments to prove a case.
- Present all sides of the question. Do not be tempted to strengthen a case by omitting divergent evidence. You are searching for the truth, not enforcing a personal opinion.
- Plagiarism can easily sneak into a review unless it is carefully avoided. Remember that plagiarism is not just using another person's words. It also includes presenting ideas as your own when they are actually from another's research source.
- You must be the sole writer of your literature review. Outside readers and editors can be very helpful, but they must maintain an advisory role and not become the authors of the research project.

The ethics disposition must stand above all other dispositions as an overriding behavior for conducting research. Ethical behavior is an essential quality of the good scientist.

REFLECTIVE OVERSIGHT

After consideration of procedure and dispositions as essential elements for critical thinking and for the work required for doing a literature review, the discussion turns to how to manage and evaluate this work. While you, the reader, might define this concept as metacognition, we are describing it as reflective oversight. By reflective oversight we mean the continuous reflection an individual uses to regulate, assess, and correct the processes used to take on a task.

Self-Regulation

Self-regulation is personal discipline used to manage and direct the quality of the work. Self-regulation can be described as considering the quality of the thinking you use when doing the work. This oversight process self-assesses and self-corrects. When engaging in a task such as a literature review, one continually reflects and monitors the procedures and thinking processes used to ensure the work's accuracy and validity.

Self-Assessment

The critical first step of self-regulation is assessment. What did I do? How did it work? These are the essential questions used when self-assessing. Self-consciously reflect on the following:

- The analytical reasoning used to verify the results produced
- The correct application of procedures and processes selected to conduct the task
- The extent to which one's thinking is influenced by deficiencies in knowledge, by stereotypes, prejudices, emotions, or any factors that constrain objectivity and rationality
- The extent to which one's dispositions influence the creation of an unbiased, fair-minded, thorough, and objective interpretation

Are my personal biases and positions affecting the accuracy of the work? Am I following quality critical-thinking procedures? Am I maintaining constructive dispositions about my work? Am I using good reasoning skills? Questions such as these are used to assess and oversee quality.

Self-Correction

The final step of self-regulation is self-correction. When self-assessment reveals deficiencies, take steps to design reasonable solutions to remedy the problem. When errors are made, correct them.

Reflective oversight is an essential aspect of the critical-thinking process. When applied to doing a literature review, it can guarantee efficiency, quality, and accuracy. More than this, reflective oversight is a learning process. The more we reflect on our actions, the more we become proficient at what we do.

Doing a literature review is a matter of procedure, disposition, and reflection. Each of these concepts is an essential element of the applied critical-thinking process used to successfully complete the work.

Before proceeding to Chapter 1, here are a number of tips that will help you become organized for the work ahead.

PLAN WISELY BEFORE YOU BEGIN

The secret of any successful journey—and a literature review *is* a kind of journey—is planning and preparation. The successful reviewer must be physically and emotionally ready and must have a plan of action. Doing a literature review well demands a commitment of focused time and effort, which will probably require a fundamental reorganization of daily life. A project such as a literature review cannot take place "when time allows" because time would probably never allow. Rather than trying to fit this new work into the already-busy day, the reviewer should seek creative solutions to reorganize the work schedule and the workplace.

First, organize a workspace free from distractions. You will need a computer with an Internet connection, copying and printing capability, notepads, writing instruments, and filing space. You will also need at least one high-quality dictionary and a thesaurus. Reference works on research methods and writing skills can also be useful. Reference tools, while available in hard copy, can now be found in abundance on the Internet and in your institution's virtual library. Plan the space and arrange it before you begin. As with any complex project, the literature review demands concentrated mental focus. Mental discipline, in turn, demands emotional balance. Make sure that your workspace supports this frame of mind.

Having a plan decreases anxiety and ambiguity. It also increases productivity. Develop a three-tiered plan. First, create an overall project plan and timeline. Second, subdivide the overall plan into sections that act as intermediate goals for the project. Finally, build daily plans from the subsections to schedule the work for each daily session. Remember, a plan implies a goal. Give yourself permission to modify your plan, but never proceed without one. Plans provide direction and organization. They build a structure to address the ambiguous and complex world of the literature review. Below are some suggestions for planning.

1. Use the literature review model, Figure I.4, to form the overall plan. First, estimate the available monthly project time. Calculate this in hours. Then, estimate the number of hours it will take to complete the tasks for each step of the literature review. If you are not comfortable assigning task times, consult with colleagues or faculty who are experienced in literature research. Next, build an overall plan and timeline for the research. Be sure to include extra time for unplanned eventualities.

2. Subdivide the plan by benchmarks that will serve as intermediate goals for the research. These benchmarks can be time or task driven. A monthly design is one choice if time is the measurement for progress. Use the steps of the literature review model if you use task completion as the measure of progress. Put the benchmarks on a timeline, and readjust the overall plan as necessary. The benchmark division drives the work. It provides a solid schedule that addresses the tasks. At this point, the work becomes tangible.

3. Build daily plans for action. Each work session must have its goals. If possible, schedule at least a 2-hour block of time for any work session. Early morning works best for many accomplished writers, allowing the reviewer to focus and concentrate more easily. Schedule quiet time with no interruptions. We recommend daily sessions. While 2-hour sessions each day may be impractical, daily work on the project is advantageous. Allowing extended time between work sessions will blur your focus. The literature review is a serious undertaking that builds one day at a time. You cannot succeed by leaving the work for the last minute. Of course, as you use the daily schedule, the benchmarks and the overall plan may need to change.

Tips

- Study the literature review model (Figure I.4). Memorize it if possible. Use this figure to keep yourself on track.
- Select a topic that is important to you. A subject of true concern or curiosity will produce better work than a topic chosen for expediency.
- Writing starts now. Write out the topic. Include in this earliest writing what you already know, or think you know, about the topic. This writing will be the beginning of the project journal. Using a computer to keep the project journal will allow for easy additions and changes as they become necessary.
- Plan each step and write it out. Completing the work diligently, and in order, takes far less time than going back to pick up missed steps.

SUMMARY

The purpose of this chapter was to provide a general introduction to both the conduct and the product of a literature review. The chapter also provided a discussion of the dispositions and reflective oversight required to guarantee the success of the project. This chapter ended with preparation tips to help launch a successful literature review. With a preliminary understanding of the project, a thoughtful mindset, and a plan, you are ready to tackle developing the research topic, which is the subject of Chapter 1.

CHECKLIST

Write your responses to the checklist below. Review what you have written for accuracy and feasibility.

Task	Completed
1. Write the definition and the purpose of a literature review.	☐
2. What general interest are you going to explore? Be specific.	☐
3. Describe your plan to use the six steps needed to create a successful literature review.	☐
4. Describe the tools and workspace you have planned. How will you create your space?	☐

REFLECTIVE OVERSIGHT

The purpose of reflective oversight is to self-correct the process covered in each chapter. Reflective oversight includes two steps. Step 1 is assessing the quality of the completed tasks listed in the checklist. Step 2 is deciding what needs to be done next. What additional skills and knowledge are necessary to correct any problems revealed by your assessment? How do you plan to acquire any necessary skills and knowledge?

1. Take some time to think carefully about this general interest. Is it of sufficient personal interest for you to devote the necessary time to pursue it?

2. After reflecting on your responses to the checklist, what do you still need to learn and do in order to move ahead?

Step 1. Select a Topic

📖 **Task 1.** Identify a Subject for Study

📖 **Task 2.** Translate the Personal Interest or Concern Into a Research Query

    ○ *Activity 1. Focus a Research Interest*

    ○ *Activity 2. Limit the Interest*

    ○ *Activity 3. Select a Perspective*

    ○ *Activity 4. Reflect and Develop the Query Statement*

📖 **Task 3.** Link the Research Query to the Appropriate Discipline

    ○ *Activity 1. Become Familiar With the Academic Terminology Concerning the Study Topic*

    ○ *Activity 2. Gain Entry to the Literature Concerning the Subject of the Study*

    ○ *Activity 3. Consult With a Research Librarian*

📖 **Task 4.** Write the Preliminary Research Topic Statement

Step One: Select a Topic

Personal Interest to Formal Research Topic

Chi zappa in fretta, raccoglierà piangendo.

Hoe in haste, harvest in tears.

The Literature Review Model

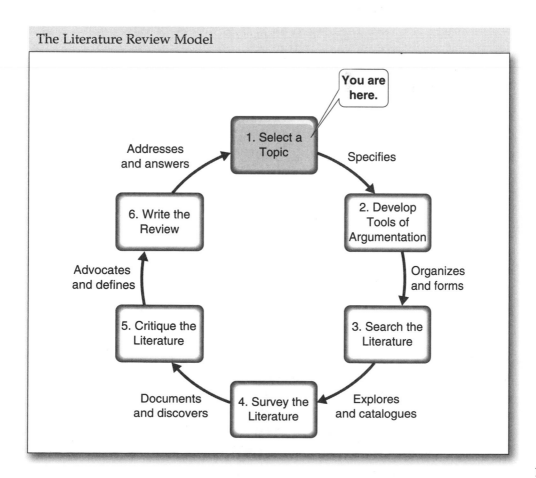

KEY VOCABULARY

- **Personal Interest or Concern**—The subject or question that provokes the need to inquire. This should not be confused with a preliminary topic.

- **Research Query**—A personal interest or concern that has been refined by focus, limit, and perspective.

- **Preliminary Topic**—A research interest statement that has been defined, limited to one subject of study, and linked to an appropriate academic discipline, enabling access to the relevant literature.

CHAPTER OVERVIEW

Recognizing and defining a subject for study is the first step of a literature review. Subjects for study in the social sciences usually originate from the conflicts, issues, concerns, or beliefs encountered in daily life. We question why some actions in the course of our work succeed while others fail, why some strategies or tactics succeed more than others, or why people think, learn, and act in certain ways. In the social sciences, our issues or concerns tend to focus on questions about individuals, groups, or organizations and seek to examine some attitude, belief, behavior, or task. These questions stem from curiosity. They stimulate the need to seek answers, to do research. Notice that when we ask these types of questions, both our emotional and our intellectual capacities are in play.

Emotions trigger a curiosity that provides the personal energy and the motivation—the *how* and *why*—to act on the question. Appropriate motivation and energy are a matter of disposition. How we are disposed will determine the effort and commitment we put toward our action. As discussed in the introduction, a proper mindset is crucial to a successful inquiry.

Our intellect identifies the subject—the *what*—of the question and directs the course of action. The *what* is defined as our **personal interest or concern**. When doing a literature review, defining and clarifying the subject—the *what* of the research—is the first order of business. The question that initially provoked our curiosity must evolve to become a suitable subject for study.

Four tasks are required to create the research topic statement. They are (1) identifying a subject for study, (2) translating this personal interest or concern into a **research query**, (3) connecting the research query to the appropriate academic discipline, and (4) writing the **preliminary topic** statement. These tasks are the subject of this chapter. Figure 1.1 illustrates this process.

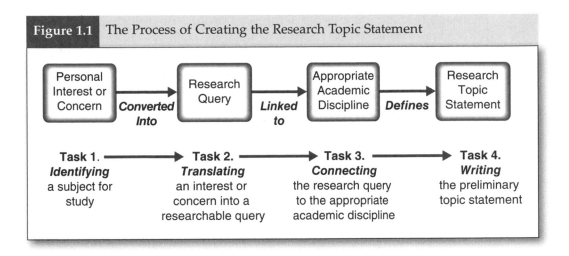

Figure 1.1 The Process of Creating the Research Topic Statement

TASK 1. IDENTIFYING A SUBJECT FOR STUDY

Most applied research in the social sciences begins by selecting an everyday problem, interest, or concern for further study. Selecting a suitable interest for research requires great care and forethought. As the opening quote of this chapter states, "Hoe in haste, harvest in tears." A hasty choice can have catastrophic consequences. Since the subject of study determines and directs the course of the work, employing good decision-making skills when making this selection is a must. A subject for study should ignite curiosity, engage emotions, and challenge thinking. Choose accordingly.

Personal reflection and introspection will uncover potential interests. Professional and public settings provide the primary context for this introspection and supply fruitful opportunities for the discovery of a possible research topic. Examples from the workplace can identify both interests and concerns. What causes the conflict among members of committee workgroups? How accurate are standardized test scores in measuring individual student achievement? These questions might target potential subjects for study.

Organizationally, each of the following questions might provide a great beginning for topic development. What is the recipe for creating successful change? Is having a forceful leader a precondition for a successful group? How does a school principal guide a teaching staff toward improving student performance?

If introspection about the workplace does not provide an interest or concern, other sources can be used. Topic suggestions can come from experts knowledgeable in academic disciplines or from skilled practitioners in the field. Seek out those professionals you respect and ask them their thoughts about potential topics.

Perhaps reading various academic and professional trade journals can provide potential subjects. Journal articles frequently suggest topics for further research.

Tapping into media and professional association reports about current issues can also uncover research alternatives. The current national, state, or local debates and initiatives concerning our professional field can produce research interests as well.

Finally, we can identify the theoretical debates occurring in a chosen academic field. Weighing into the debate by applying applicable theory to argue the issue can very well be a subject for research. What theories in cognitive psychology speak to the developmental learning abilities of students? What does sociological theory predict about group behavior? How does theory in cultural anthropology provide an understanding of the culture of the work community? Theoretical models in the various social sciences can always provide new insights to both practical and theoretical questions. Potential subjects of study abound here.

The following is a list of possible resources to assist in identifying a subject for study:

- Professional experience
- Suggestions from experts
- Academic journals
- Topical debates within your profession
- Examining academic theory in your field

Exercises

Exercises are found throughout this text to help in the various tasks of developing a literature review. The first four exercises in this chapter will employ free writes. A *free write* is spontaneous writing done without reference to notes or outlines. Its purpose is to explore what you have already internalized about a subject. These exercises will lead you through the four tasks using free writes; one will appear at the end of each of this chapter's subsections. The subject statement for each exercise is followed by guiding questions to help you free write. Respond to each question by writing ideas as they occur to you.

The following guiding questions will help specify your interests and reveal your personal attachments. These questions should enable you to pinpoint an interest and recognize your personal connection with the interest you wish to study.

Use a separate page for each session. Write the topic and the questions for that exercise at the head of the paper. Then, answer each question in descending order. Read the question aloud and then act quickly, allowing ideas and written responses to flow. As ideas come to mind, write them as simple, independent, declarative statements, one after the other, as quickly as possible. Do not be concerned with spelling, grammar, or composition.

Allow no more than about 15 minutes for each session. If you have exhausted your responses to the questions before the end of 15 minutes, wait for about 30 seconds and then push yourself to find three more responses. After the exercise, leave the page, without reading it, for about a day. At the end of the 24-hour period, go back to your writing for that exercise. Read, review, edit, delete, and add whatever comes to mind. Follow this pattern for the exercise in each of the next four subsections.

EXERCISE 1.1

Discovering the Subject of Your Interest or Issue of Concern

1. What is your personal interest or issue?
2. What are the component parts of this interest?
3. Why did you become curious about this question?

Researcher Bias, Note Well

Researchers have opinions about the problems in their field and often have pet viewpoints to which they are committed. These preconceptions and personal attachments are both strengths and weaknesses in a research effort. Personal attachment to an interest provides the passion and dedication necessary for conducting good research, which is a plus. However, personal attachment can also carry bias and opinion, causing researchers to jump to premature conclusions. Rather than arriving at a conclusion based on methodical scholarly work, it is easy to succumb to bias. While bias and opinion can never be removed completely, they must be recognized and controlled.

How does a researcher control bias and opinion? First, careful introspection can bring these personal views forward, where they can be identified for what they are. By rationally identifying and confronting these views, the researcher can control personal bias and opinion and commit to being open-minded, skeptical, and considerate of research data. If these attachments remain embedded and unidentified, the research can be severely compromised. A researcher hobbled by unchecked bias can only produce biased findings.

EXERCISE 1.2

Understanding the Personal Viewpoint

1. What previous knowledge do you have about your interest?

2. What personal experience do you have that influences you about this issue or interest?

3. What are your beliefs, biases, and opinions about this interest or issue?

4. What predisposes you to certain conclusions about the issue or concern of study?

5. How will you identify and isolate your personal bias, opinion, feelings, and intuition to preserve a neutral position as a researcher?

This exercise should have uncovered some caveats. Preconceived ideas are unavoidable but must not be allowed to control or influence the research. They can, however, be a point of entry to the significance—the *why*—of the research.

TASK 2. TRANSLATING THE PERSONAL INTEREST OR CONCERN INTO A RESEARCH QUERY

After successfully identifying a personal interest or concern as a subject for study, turn to Task 2.

Consider which of these two statements would be easier to research: "How does the weather change from season to season?" Or, "To what degree is March weather in coastal northern California influenced by an Arctic flow of air?" The second statement plainly works better because it provides clear definition of the subject. A clear definition allows a direct path to the available literature. Early considerations of a research interest are often stated too broadly. They lack subject focus, limitation, and perspective and are, at best, ill defined.

Activity 1. Focusing a Research Interest

When asked to select a research interest, most beginning researchers will provide a generalized statement. One such statement might be, "To what degree do standardized test scores predict actual student achievement?" The problem with this example is its lack of specificity. Given this statement as presented, could a researcher see and measure the concern? Of course not. The interest, as expressed, is too broad. Its terms are not clearly defined.

The subject of any interest is defined by its key ideas, those words and phrases creating its meaning. A too-broad interest statement tends to be ambiguous and wordy, in need of precise definition. A hazy interest statement may contain assumptions and inferences that must be clarified. Broad scope and lack of a clear description of key ideas demand revision to sharpen the focus necessary to access the literature.

Examine the question about standardized tests scores stated earlier. What are its key ideas? To identify them, look first for the subjects, verbs, and objects of the sentence. In this interest statement, the subject is *scores*, the verb is *predict*, and the object is *achievement*. These are the key ideas to be examined. When taking apart this interest statement, it quickly becomes clear that this subject is too broad. What type of scores? What content do these test scores assess? What does the verb *predict* mean? How can we measure it? What does the object *achievement* mean? This interest needs to be more precisely defined. If the subject statement is ambiguous, the researcher cannot identify the actual subject of the review. Developing exact definitions for each of the key ideas that make up the interest statement brings the statement into focus. Once the subject is in focus, we need to ensure its topic is limited.

Activity 2. Limiting the Interest

The second refinement limits the subject of our interest. Limiting the interest means narrowing the study to one clearly defined subject. Does this interest contain multiple subjects for study? You must choose one subject to study, one that can be examined clearly.

Broad interests often contain multiple subjects that could be studied, each of which could provide important contributions. The trick is to settle on one interest. "I am interested in why students are not achieving," is one such case. This interest could be studied from an individual, group, or organizational perspective. For instance, the research perspective could focus on the student, specifically on individual student behavior, attitude, skills, or knowledge. How can a change in student behavior affect performance on an achievement test? How do student attitudes affect performance in certain achievement assessments? Alternatively, the research perspective could focus on group behavior. How does a certain group respond to certain testing conditions? What are the effects of this kind of test on group performance? From an organizational viewpoint, a researcher might ask what effect providing pretest review time has on individual student achievement scores.

After limiting the broad interest, usable topic questions appear, such as, "To what degree are state standardized test scores in language arts predictive of individual student success in college placement with regard to Subject A exams?" Or, "How does teacher competency in test preparation of students affect student achievement on a standardized test?"

EXERCISE 1.3

Limiting the Interest of Your Study

Remember to write your answers in detail so that you end up with a useful reference page.

1. Clearly identify the subject of the study interest.

2. Are you looking at individuals, groups, or organizations?

3. Specifically name the individuals, groups, or organizations that you plan to study.

The above exercise probably produced many choices for possible research focuses. The next step is to select one of the possible subjects for study.

Activity 3. Selecting a Perspective

Once the subject focus is selected, choose the perspective or vantage point—the place from which to view the subject. What perspective most appropriately fits the query? Choice of perspective depends on the subject chosen for study and the unit of analysis from which the researcher has chosen to study it. What is the unit of analysis? Is this a study of individuals, groups, or organizations/communities? The unit of analysis is important because social science theory is divided in this way. The subject's unit of analysis must be linked to the appropriate academic discipline to gain access to the pertinent information about the subject.

To illustrate this point, a researcher might study the communal behavior of groups and the effects this has on standardized testing and student achievement. Perhaps the researcher might address the social interactions that affect student achievement. If the subject is defined from the individual student's perspective, then psychology may provide the best vantage point. If the subject focuses on a community perspective, then cultural anthropology may provide the best vantage point. If the subject is achievement from the perspective of group reactions and interactions, then sociology may provide the best vantage point. As with the focus, the researcher must narrow the perspective. Probably choices surfaced from the previous exercise. Select the discipline and unit of analysis that present the best perspective for accessing data about the subject of study.

Clearly defined key ideas, a limitation of subject, and the perspective for study transform a broad personal interest into an acceptable research query.

EXERCISE 1.4

Choosing the Perspective for the Study

1. What academic fields best lend themselves to your subject and perspective for research? (If you are still considering more than one perspective, choose a suitable academic field for each perspective.)

2. What are the specific knowledge areas of this academic field that will best help in exploring and defining the research subject?

3. What knowledge competency do you have in this academic field?

4. What additional knowledge of this academic field do you need to acquire to have a solid foundation to address this interest?

Activity 4. Reflection: The Key to Interest Selection and Developing the Research Query Statement

The key to developing a successful research topic is the ability to examine the personal interest, concern, or problem to study. The more clarity and specificity brought to bear in defining the interest, the easier it is to connect this interest to a researchable topic of study.

Experience with students choosing interests tells us that beginning researchers sometimes neglect to take the time necessary to reflect on what they will actually study. Selecting an interest of study haphazardly without considering intent, perspective, or vantage point can produce awkward and unsatisfactory results. Therefore, taking time to carefully choose an interest for study is essential for all researchers.

Taking a personal interest and transforming it into a usable research query is much like setting up a photograph. Compare selecting a subject for research to photographing a scene. Imagine yourself standing at Big Rock Campground in Joshua Tree National Park. Around you are miles of desert with shifting light and shadow. Perhaps there are also people, reptiles, plants, or insects in your scene. Do you want a photo of an ancient juniper tree, or do you want a picture of a family around a campfire? What is the purpose of the photograph, and what is your goal? If your goal is to record the entire park through time, you would have a lifetime's work. Usually, though, the intent is not to photograph the entire park or to study everything about a subject from all perspectives. Instead it is to select one worthy subject of interest and to do it justice using your chosen perspective.

For both the photographer and the researcher, an initial interest in a subject triggers the task. In both cases, we have a specific image of the outcome that we expect to see. Also in both cases, that early expectation will, in all likelihood, be different from what actually results. The selection of the subject of a photograph is just a starting point. A satisfactory end product will appear only after much exploration into focus, intent, and perspective, all of which will change as you delve deeper into the subject. Perhaps the final photo will be substantially different from what was originally conceived. In both photography and research, it is necessary to be willing to see what actually works and to continue down productive paths and abandon those paths that meander aimlessly without leading to satisfactory results. The first photograph may be of a jagged rock, but the photo you keep may be a close-up of the quartz fragments in one section of metamorphic stone in that jagged rock.

Like a photographer, a researcher must have a subject of interest that launches the inquiry and must also craft and mold the result. The researcher follows a path that works to define the research interest rather than simply adhering to the original intent. Evidence, whether of the eye or the mind, must lead the way.

EXERCISE 1.5

Developing Your Research Query Statement

This exercise combines and patterns the information gathered from your free writes. Reflect on and analyze the written information produced by the earlier exercises and develop a specific statement of interest. Initially, this statement could be a single question or the research query statement. Make it clear and concise. Develop a second statement that defines the significance of the research. Finally, write a statement that clearly defines the beliefs, values, biases, and opinions relating to your research and note how you will accommodate them.

Using the information you have acquired through your introspective work in Exercises 1.1 through 1.4, answer the following three questions:

1. What is your specific personal interest?

    a. The interest, issue, or concern of my research is _____. (Answer in seven sentences.)

    b. Cross out the two least important sentences without changing the key idea.

    c. Cross out any words or phrases that can be removed without changing the meaning.

    d. Reduce your remaining draft to three sentences.

    e. Be sure your final three sentences identify the subject (what you are studying), perspective (how you are looking at it), and vantage point (which academic field you are using).

2. What contributions to the field make this research important?

3. What are your beliefs, values, biases, and opinions about this interest?

   a. How will these beliefs, values, biases, and opinions help you in conducting your research?

   b. How will you prevent the beliefs and biases contained in your personal viewpoint from affecting the necessary neutral stance of a researcher?

Now, using your answers for Questions 1 through 3, write a statement that clearly defines the interest for your research work, a statement that defines the significance of your research, and a statement that defines your personal tendencies and how you will control them. When completed, you will have a researchable interest.

TASK 3. LINK THE RESEARCH QUERY TO THE APPROPRIATE DISCIPLINE

Now it is time to address the last concern of this chapter: refining the personal interest of a study statement into a suitable topic for formal research. Begin by reviewing your progress so far.

Figure 1.1, introduced earlier in the chapter, provides the four tasks for creating an acceptable topic for research. Reading from left to right, notice that in Task 1 we selected an interest that we identified as a subject for study. We focused the interest by clarifying and defining its **core ideas**. We limited the interest to one subject. Then in Task 2 we chose a perspective—a link to a specific discipline—to access the pertinent literature. We created a research query statement. Now it is time to reword the personal interest statement using the language of the chosen academic perspective.

When addressing Task 3 of Figure 1.1, we leave personal understanding and turn our attention to the shared knowledge about the subject provided by the academic community. To accomplish this task, align the research interest statement with the external concern and work of that academic community. Why is this important? Without aligning the research interest to the topic of study as addressed by the academic community, there is no avenue or language to gain access and entry to the relevant academic body of knowledge.

Some students believe having a well-defined personal interest statement provides sufficient topic definition to proceed directly into research. These students then complain that they searched the Internet, spent hours in the library, and exhausted the library's online resources. They worked hard at gathering information about their topic but could find nothing written on it. These students were using their everyday vocabulary to access the specific language, vocabulary, and discourse of a specialized field.

Rarely does a researcher stumble onto a unique and previously unidentified topic of study. Previous work has been done on almost all of the interests under consideration. So what is the difficulty? The difficulty is a lack of linkage between the wording of subject definition and appropriate academic terms of the academic discipline. Word usage and meaning are particular to context. All academic fields have an esoteric language to describe their subjects of study. The chances are remote that a researcher's use of everyday language conforms to the technical language an academic field uses.

Consider the word *conflict*. Informally, *conflict* is defined as a disagreement or argument, or as an incompatibility of goals between parties. As used in the discipline of history, *conflict* could mean a war, as in an armed conflict. As used in organizational psychology, *conflict* is an organizational breakdown of the standard mechanisms of decision making. As used in social psychology, *conflict* is behavior that occurs when two or more parties are in disagreement. As used in personal psychology, *conflict* may refer to a person's internal struggle. As used in literature, *conflict* is whatever keeps a character from achieving a goal. Each academic discipline defines terms to meet its specific needs.

You must study the specialized vocabulary of the academic field chosen and become familiar with the terminology that identifies the potential subject of study. Once functionally skilled in the appropriate language, a researcher can easily translate the key ideas that provide subject definition and topic definition for the subject of study.

Three activities must be accomplished in order to complete Task 3. They are (1) becoming familiar with the academic terminology, (2) gaining entry into the discourse about the intended subject of study, and (3) consulting with a research librarian (Figure 1.2).

Figure 1.2	Task 3: Converting the Research Interest Into a Preliminary Topic Statement

Job	Purpose	References*	Library Access	Virtual Library Access
Activity 1	Become familiar with the academic terminology	Subject-area thesauri and dictionaries	In reference stacks, cataloged by academic discipline	Either: Do a keyword search. Query by keyword, by particular reference type, or by availability online. Or: Query *Library A–Z* on the main page of the library Web site. Reference types will be in alphabetical order.
Activity 2	Gain entry into the discourse about the intended subject of study	Subject-area encyclopedias and handbooks		
Activity 3	Consult with a research librarian			

---

* The reference texts used in Task 3 are particular to a specific academic discipline. Thesauri, dictionaries, encyclopedias, and handbooks are compiled for each social science discipline. Seek out the appropriate ones. Do not use generic references for this task.

The reference section of the library provides the necessary tools to easily complete the jobs of Task 3. Refer to Figure 1.2. For Activity 1, begin by consulting the *subject-area thesauri and dictionaries* to become familiar with the academic terminology that fits the interest statement. Each of these references has a particular purpose. Use a *subject-area thesaurus* to find the synonyms that link appropriate academic terminology to the keywords of the interest statement. When using this reference, you may also find particular words that better define and narrow the topic of study.

The *subject-area dictionary* provides a different reference point. Using the results of the thesaurus search, consult these specialized dictionaries to determine if the definition of the terms selected fits your needs. It is important to note here that by querying subject-area dictionaries and thesauri, we find the language used by the academic discipline to define the topic. These references provide the language familiarity and phrasing necessary to transform the terms of the interest statement into a viable preliminary topic statement, a statement aligned to the chosen academic field. Once you have identified the correct terms that correspond to your interest, you have completed Activity 1.

Using the newly found terminology, consult the *subject-area handbooks and encyclopedias* to access the academic discourse about the topic. *Subject-area handbooks* discuss the theories relating to the topics of their academic field. They provide a great head start in determining the boundaries for the literature search and in creating an overview of the academic discourse about the subject.

Subject-area handbooks can be organized in three ways. First, handbooks can discuss theory as it evolves. This is done chronologically. A theory is first discussed, and as it changes, the commentary evolves. Second, theories can be organized topically. In this case, you find the research topic that aligns to your needs and review the section for the appropriate discussion about that theory. Third, handbooks may be organized around current discussions in the field. This type of handbook deals with the hot topics in the academic area and emerging theoretical considerations.

Subject-area encyclopedias also provide great access to the academic discourse on the subject. Because encyclopedias are organized in alphabetical order, it is easy to find the theory and discussion relating to a specific topic. Using the keywords and terms selected from Activity 1, simply page to the reference point in the encyclopedia and read on. The encyclopedic entry will begin with an overview of the subject, followed by a detailed discussion of relevant theory. Lastly, the entry will list the relevant contributors and authors for further study.

After consulting the appropriate subject-area encyclopedias and handbooks, you will have translated the everyday language of the interest statement into the terminology of an academic field. You also have an overview of the topic and the relevant theory and discourse about the topic. Finally, you have built a beginning list of the theories and contributing authors in order to begin the literature search. Activity 2 is complete.

Just a word about where to find these important reference tools in the library: When going to a university library, find the reference section or reference stacks. The reference books will be cataloged by academic discipline. Seek out the appropriate discipline for your interest and find the references that address the topic.

There are two basic options to use when consulting the library's virtual portal. First, do a keyword search. This query will request three pieces of information: (1) keyword, (2) the particular reference text category, and (3) the library location, which, in this case, is online. For instance, if you are looking for dictionaries, type in *keyword, dictionaries, virtual online.* This query will display all of the reference dictionaries available online. Simply select the academic discipline dictionaries appropriate to your perspective and you are on your way. The second option can usually be found on the main page of the virtual library portal. It is a subject "hot button" called *Library A–Z.* When clicking this hot button, a new screen will appear providing an alphabetical listing of all the resources in the virtual library. Scroll down to the reference category needed and click it. All of those references will be displayed. Say you are looking for handbooks. Click *Library A–Z* on the main page of the library portal. An alphabetical listing of the library resources will appear. Scroll down to the *H* section of the listing, find *Handbooks,* and click that entry. All of the handbooks available will appear, and you can sort through them to determine the appropriate entries for the review.

By using the new language and definitions found when completing Activities 1 and 2, you have now linked and translated the interest statement into the vocabulary of the academic discipline. Now it is time to seek advice. Make an appointment with the university's research librarian. Consultation can be done at a university library or online, as available. The purpose is to discuss the research interest as it has now developed. Look for confirmation about your thinking, a critical review of the interest statement, and tips and advice.

Rules for Library Use: A Primer

Before your first trip to the library, whether you are consulting online resources (a virtual library) or an actual library, stop for a minute and review some important rules on library use. Heeding these rules will save time and produce better results.

Rule 1. Know Your Librarian

- The research librarian, whether online or in person, is a friend, a guide, and a coach. When using a library for the first time, consult first with a research librarian. Make sure that you have formed a positive relationship and can rely on the librarian as coach, mentor, and confidant.

Rule 2. Be Purposeful

- Have a clear purpose and plan when researching. Wandering the stacks, exploring the subject catalog, or surfing Web sites is entertaining, but it is not productive.
- Every time you conduct research, know what you are looking for and where to get it.
- Have a strategy for research. Planning saves time. Know what you want to do before you take your first step. What types of information do you need, and where can they be found? Are you scanning the subject catalogs to refine your topic? Are you consulting the specific subject dictionaries to define terms?
- Have a schedule of work and specific outcomes in mind for the visit. Set goals and stick to them. Brick-and-mortar and online libraries present many temptations and distractions—a provocative title that catches the eye, a new book from a favorite author, an enticing reference link. You must be disciplined. Honor your time, schedule your breaks, and focus on the task.
- Finally, before ending a session, plan the next tasks. What work must be done next? What is the timeline? What new resources do you need? Address these questions as part of a debriefing with your written notes. Remember, we have short memories. Waiting to write notes later invites ambiguity and misdirection.

Rule 3. Remember That Preparation Equals Efficiency

- Be prepared. Develop and organize cataloging and documenting tools before beginning a research session.
- Use cataloging to codify the library materials you have accessed in such a way that you can easily refer back to them and can properly identify them by the library indexing system for further reference. Cataloging tools range from simple 3x5 index cards to research software tools. RefWorks is available on most university Web sites, or you can purchase software such as EndNote or Citation.
- Know that documentation tools are repositories of notable information. They can store notes about a subject, quotes and abstracts, further references to explore, subject maps, or a list of tasks to be completed next. Documentation tools contain library data collected for study. These tools also have various levels of sophistication, the simplest being a notebook or notepad. The more complex and integrated ones are software such as EndNote, Citation, Microsoft OneNote, ISI ResearchSoft Reference Manager, or RefWorks.
- Take the time before you begin researching to build an organizational system that fits your learning style and will aid you through the entire literature review. Organizing now will save much time and heartache later.

TASK 4. WRITE THE PRELIMINARY RESEARCH TOPIC STATEMENT

Now you have the necessary information to complete Task 4: writing the preliminary research topic statement. Using the new language and definitions found when completing Task 3, rewrite the interest statement. Review the reframed statement to determine if it adequately addresses the intent of your interest. If so, you have now constructed a preliminary topic statement for your study. If not, rework and revise the study's focus and vantage point, or search the reference works further for other terms that would better suit your interest. Use these options until you are satisfied that the preliminary topic statement aligns with the original interest statement. Task 4 has been accomplished. You are now ready to learn about argumentation.

The following exercise will guide you through the task of transforming the formal interest statement written in Exercise 1.1 into a preliminary topic of research. It requires you to complete the following:

- Conduct a first conversation with a research librarian.
- Define the key terms of the interest statement.
- Translate the key terms and core ideas of the interest statement.
- Rewrite the interest statement into a preliminary topic statement.

EXERCISE 1.6

Refining Your Research Topic Statement

1. Conduct a first conversation with a research librarian.

   a. Make an appointment with a research librarian or connect with your school's online librarian. Explain your research project. Provide your interest statement to the librarian for review and advice. You may also want to confer with your research faculty adviser or other faculty member for coaching on the formal research interest statement.

   b. When talking to the research librarian, review your interest statement. State the perspective and academic vantage point chosen for your interest. Seek advice on the clarity and specificity of your work. If the librarian does not understand your interest as stated, go back to Exercise 1.5 and reframe the interest based on that information.

   c. Ask the librarian to provide a survey of the library. Get the specifics of the inner workings of the reference section, stacks and holdings, periodicals, cataloging system, search capacities, and Internet access. Pay particular attention to the library's ability to address the academic field chosen for the study and the stated research interest. If you need more resources to complete your study, consult with the librarian.

    d. Review the key terms and core ideas contained in your interest statement. Ask the librarian how to access the subject-area dictionaries, encyclopedias, handbooks, and other reference books that address these terms and ideas. This can be done in person or online.

2. Define the key terms of the interest statement.

    a. Using the key terms, consult the chosen subject-area dictionaries, encyclopedias, and handbooks. Find the technical definitions of your key terms.

    b. Rewrite the interest statement using the technical terms of that academic field.

    c. Review the reframed statement. Does it still express your intended interest? If it does not, rework and revise the study's focus and vantage point, or search the reference works further for other terminology to use until the reframed statement expresses your research interest.

    d. When the reframed statement works, go to Number 3.

3. Translate the key terms and core ideas of the interest statement.

    a. Taking your reframed interest statement, search the subject-area encyclopedias, handbooks, yearbooks, and other reference materials for topic areas that address the core ideas contained in your reframed interest. Rewrite as the topic of your study.

    b. Document and catalog the results, noting prevalent authors and theory.

    c. Begin to build subject and author maps for each of the core ideas in the interest statement.

    d. Review your work. Check for accuracy and understanding.

4. Rewrite the interest statement as the preliminary topic of your study.

Tips

1. Make sure your interest is specific. Reflect on the key terms that make up your interest statement. Be sure that you clearly understand what the key terms mean and how they interact.

2. Focus the interest to ensure that it is clearly described and singularly defined.

3. Select an academic perspective and translate the key terms to those used in that academic field.

4. Approach research with an open mind.

5. Document, document, document.

SUMMARY

You now have the preliminary topic for study. You have successfully conducted personal introspection to identify an interest, and you have refined that interest as a potential subject suitable for study. You are now ready to learn about argumentation. While the work seems linear, it is not. Notice that in Figure 1.1 the personal interest informs the research query. The opposite also holds true. The research query informs the personal interest. The thinking needed to unmask the specific ideas in one of these statements requires knowledge of the other. The deep or fundamental understanding of one refines the understanding of the other. So it is with a research query and the academic discipline knowledge base. The more you learn about the topic through initial reading in the literature, the more refined the topic becomes. Refinement is an essential part of subject exploration and topic definition.

CHECKLIST

Task	Completed
1. Write a clear, specific description of your personal interest.	☐
2. Define the key concepts and terms contained in your area of interest.	☐
3. Reread your interest statement to check that you are studying only one subject. Is the subject too broad or too narrow?	☐
4. Select an academic perspective, a specific field of study that aligns with your research subject.	☐
5. Become familiar with the resources and the structure of your library. Engage a research librarian in an introductory session regarding the subject of study.	☐
6. Prepare documenting tools.	☐
7. Rewrite the research query statement as a preliminary topic statement using the correct academic terms.	☐

REFLECTIVE OVERSIGHT

1. Did I identify an appropriate subject?

2. Is my subject of interest researchable?

3. Have I connected appropriately to an academic discipline?

4. Does my preliminary topic statement reflect what I want to do, and is it relevant and significant to the academic discipline?

Step 2. Develop the Tools of Argumentation

Step Two: Develop the Tools of Argumentation

Making the Case for the Literature Review

Quod erat demonstrandum

[That] which was to be demonstrated (QED)

The Literature Review Model

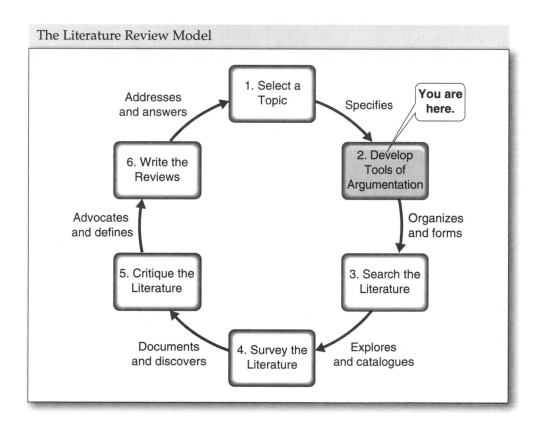

KEY VOCABULARY

- **Argument**—The presentation of one or more claims backed by credible evidence that supports a logical conclusion.

- **Argument of Advocacy**—Argument based on claims that have been proven as fact and that serve as the premises for logically driving a conclusion—in this case, the thesis statement of the literature review.

- **Argument of Discovery**—Argument proving that the findings of fact represent the current state of knowledge regarding the research topic.

- **Claim**—A declaration of a proposed truth that is open to challenge.

- **Evidence**—A set of data presented as the grounds for substantiating a claim.

- **Warrant**—The reasoning used in an argument to allow the researcher and any reader to accept the evidence presented as reasonable proof that the position of the claim is correct.

CHAPTER OVERVIEW

At this point, the research topic has been defined and a clear path has been laid out for collecting data. The understandable urge now is to plunge into the literature search and begin reviewing the literature. But while the topic—the *what*—of the literature review is clearly defined, the *how* is still undefined. How does one build an acceptable literature review? Proceeding into the review process without a clear understanding of the *how* is surely a path to disaster.

Critical thinking would suggest that before a problem such as a literature review can be solved, one must have a way to solve it. Consider this simple question as an example of what is meant by this: "I am holding up two fingers on one hand and two fingers on the other. How many fingers am I holding up?" This problem cannot be solved unless the process of addition of numbers is understood and employed. What problem-solving process needs to be employed to produce a quality literature review? Clear criteria are found in the definition of a literature review, as presented in the introductory chapter:

> *A literature review is a written document that presents a logically argued case founded on a comprehensive understanding of the current state of knowledge about a topic of study. This case establishes a convincing thesis to answer the study's question.*

A *logically argued case* must be made to produce an acceptable literature review. The pathway—the *how*—to do a literature review now becomes clear. It is a process of argumentation. How does one argue a case about the topic of study that establishes a *convincing thesis to answer the study's question?* The answer to this question is the subject of this chapter.

Chapter 2 presents the foundational concepts necessary for building a case. These concepts cover the elements for making a logical argument. The chapter begins by explaining how arguments are made to build a case. It continues by defining the essential elements of any simple logical argument, followed by a detailed explanation of each element. The chapter concludes with a discussion of how a complex argument is constructed.

Apply the conceptual knowledge you learn from this chapter when working on the remaining steps of the literature review process. You might consider referring back to this chapter and using it as a process guide for the review.

CONCEPT 1. BUILDING THE CASE FOR A LITERATURE REVIEW

Building a case means compiling and arranging sets of facts in a logical fashion to prove the thesis made about the research topic. For example, if a thesis states participatory leadership is the most effective style for leading a 21st-century organization, the data in the literature review must support and prove this conclusion. The following simple example demonstrates how to build the case for a literature review:

Picture an evening in early spring, when changing weather patterns are unpredictable. You are deciding what to wear to work tomorrow. Should you dress for rain? You look at the newspaper and see that the forecast is for rain. You check the barometer and find the pressure steadily falling. You look outside and see that cloud formations are building. You check online and see that storms are predicted for the next few days. Considering all the information gathered, you conclude there is a high likelihood for rain tomorrow. You also decide that the available data indicate the rainstorm will probably hit during your morning commute. You apply the results of this research to your question, "What do I wear to work tomorrow?" and decide to wear a raincoat and take an umbrella.

Notice that two conclusions are present in the example. The initial conclusion is, "Rain is likely." This first conclusion was derived using different sources to gather and combine information about weather conditions. The argument for this conclusion was made by analyzing information from different sources and deciding that rain was imminent. Using this conclusion, it now becomes possible to address the question of whether to dress for rain. The second conclusion is, "I should dress for rain." The argument for this conclusion was built by interpreting the first conclusion, "Rain is likely." The results and conclusions of the first argument were applied as the basis for the second. These results reasoned that rain was approaching and that wearing a raincoat and carrying an umbrella would be the most prudent course of action.

How does the rain example apply to writing a literature review? In preparing a literature review, one must present similarly developed arguments to make the research case. An **argument** is the logical presentation of evidence that leads to and justifies a conclusion. The literature review uses two arguments to make its case.

The first argument is an **inductive argument**. Called the **argument of discovery**, its function is to discuss and explain what is known about the subject in question. When building the argument of discovery, gather the data about the subject, analyze it, and develop findings that present the current state of knowledge about the research topic. For example, if the interest is to determine the ideal leadership style for organizations in the 21st century, then the information to be discovered must provide the evidence to argue what is known about leadership styles.

The argument of discovery serves as the foundation for the second argument, an implicative argument, called the **argument of advocacy**. The function of the argument of advocacy is to analyze and critique the knowledge gained from the discovery argument to answer the research question. The answer to this argument is the thesis statement (initially discussed in the introductory chapter).

Continuing with the leadership style example, let's say the discovery argument produced findings that documented many leadership styles and their effective uses. The advocacy argument must use these findings to determine which, if any, of these styles meets the needs of a 21st-century organization. The conclusion, based on the evidence the case presents, is that the participatory leadership style is best in the specific situation named. This conclusion—"a participatory leadership style is the best fit for a 21st-century organization"—becomes the thesis statement. The two types of arguments are presented in detail in the chapters on Step 4 and Step 5. Now the basic rules for making arguments and building cases need to be examined.

CONCEPT 2. ARGUMENTS—THE BASICS

When considering the word *argument*, you probably think of two people engaged in a dispute. Each is trying to overpower the other's belief, using arguments based on opinion, bias, belief, or emotions. These reasons, however, do not provide a legitimate foundation for a research argument. As seen in the introductory chapter, the use of the rational, persuasive argument is the stock-in-trade of the researcher. This type of argument uses reasoned discussion or debate to separate fact from fiction. Scholarly argumentation is not meant to overpower, but rather to persuade and convince. The persuasive argument is logical. It presents a set of claims backed by sound reasons to support a conclusion. The reasons provided build on solid evidence.

The rules of the persuasive argument are simple: If valid reasons are presented that logically justify the conclusion, the argument is sound. If the reasons are not convincing, or if the logic applied fails to support the conclusion, the conclusion is unsound. Here is a simple formula:

An argument = reason$_a$ + reason$_b$ + . . . reason$_n$ ∴ conclusion.

Apply this formula to the weather example presented earlier. Clouds are gathering (*reason$_a$*), the barometer is falling (*reason$_b$*), and rain is forecast (*reason$_c$*); therefore, it will probably rain during the morning commute. "It will rain on our commute" is the thesis of our argument (*conclusion*).

CONCEPT 3. EVALUATING THE BASIC PARTS OF AN ARGUMENT

The following four questions provide a handy guide for checking the validity of an argument. Ask these questions whenever you are evaluating an argument.

1. What is the stated conclusion?

2. What are the reasons that support the conclusion?

3. Do the reasons stated have convincing data to support them?

4. Does the conclusion logically follow from those reasons?

A persuasive argument can come in many patterns and can employ sets of reasons formed into logical constructions of many sorts. The types of evidence and supporting data making up each reason can vary as well. However, regardless of the number of reasons presented, the evidence supplied, and the logical reasoning used, the case made must logically justify the conclusion reached. Figure 2.1 diagrams the simple argument.

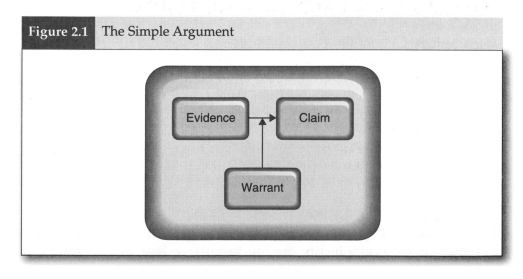

Figure 2.1 The Simple Argument

Notice that Figure 2.1 contains the essential parts of a simple argument: the evidence, the claim, and the warrant. **Claims** are declarations of a proposed truth. **Evidence** consists of data that define and support the claim. At the intersection of evidence and claim is the **warrant**. It represents the logical formation of the claims and evidence and is the glue that holds claims and evidence together. The warrant employs a line of logic that justifies accepting the claim. The warrant is the *because* statement. Usually it is indirect (implied), although it can be direct. For example,

- You should not cross the street. (Claim)
- The signal light is red. (Evidence)
- The unstated rule implies that a red signal light means stop. (Warrant)

The simple argument represents the basic building block for making the research case.

Now that you have a general understanding of a simple argument (Figure 2.1), it is time to examine each part of the simple argument in depth. Claims, evidence, and warrants are the subjects for the remainder of this chapter.

EXERCISE 2.1

A Guided Practice

Review the following arguments using the three questions presented with Concept 3. Write your answers to the three evaluating questions and check your answers against ours, which follow each numbered argument.

Argument 1. Teamwork is necessary to get the job done.

Jobs are only completed when teamwork is present. Teamwork and job completion go hand in hand. When groups act as teams, they succeed.

If you analyze Argument 1, applying Question 1, you find four conclusions: (1) teamwork is necessary, (2) completing jobs requires teamwork, (3) teamwork and job completion go hand in hand, and (4) groups acting as teams succeed. These four conclusions are redundant. When you ask the second and third questions, you find that no reasons are present to support the conclusion. Without reasons, there is no argument for the conclusion. The conclusion is unsupported.

Argument 2. Teamwork is necessary to get the job done because individuals need to get their way to be productive.

Individuals need to work independently of one another to produce good work. The central responsibility of a team is to allow all of its members their own space. Research suggests that individual identity is necessary for a group to remain cohesive. It further suggests that individual identity prevents groupthink and that individuality is the basis for creative work.

When you apply the three questions to Argument 2, you are left with ambiguous conclusions. When you ask the first question, you cannot be sure whether the conclusion is, "Teamwork is necessary to get the job done," or if it is, "Individuals need to work independently of one another to produce good work." When you ask the second question, you find some reasons to support the conclusion that independent action of a group member is essential to group productivity. No data are present, however, to support the reasoning. Finally, when you ask the third question, the reasons given do not support the conclusion. If "teamwork is necessary to get the job done" is the conclusion, the reasons support something different. Argument 2 is not sound.

Argument 3. Teamwork is necessary for a long-term work group to be successful in the group task.

We draw this conclusion based on the following research:

> Study X found that when work groups engaged in group problem solving and collaboration, group communications and productivity increased. Study Y found that when groups engaged in productive interpersonal team skills and behaviors, group performance increased. Study Z measured team development based on individual member understanding of group mission, coordination, and unity. This study found that when these qualities were present in a positive sense, they were predictive of high group performance and productivity.

Argument 3 states a conclusion in the first sentence, thus answering Question 1. The support for this conclusion is cited research. When examining each of the studies, you find that they support the conclusion drawn, thus answering Question 2. When reviewing Question 3, we find that the reasons stated are logical and convincing. All the parts of an argument are in order here, and Argument 3 is sound.

Building an argument is simple. Before you arrive at a conclusion, be sure you can justify it.

CONCEPT 4. UNDERSTANDING CLAIMS

Claims

The claim is the argument's assertion. It drives the argument. In a persuasive argument, the claim is a declarative statement. A claim asserts a position, an idea that is put forth for consideration and acceptance. The claim made in the weather example was, "Dress for rain."

Chris Hart (2001a), in his text *Doing a Literature Review,* suggests that claims are classified into five types: claims of (1) fact, (2) worth, (3) policy, (4) concept, and (5) interpretation.

Claims of Fact

Claims of fact are statements of proposed truth about a person, place, or thing. Claims of this type are the most often used when building the arguments for a literature review. The following are examples of claims of fact:

- California ranks 49th among the 50 states in its funding for public education.
- Trans-fatty acids in foods are a major contributor to a high cholesterol count.

Claims of fact must be justified by factual evidence—evidence of truth.

Claims of Worth

Claims of worth propose judgments on the merit of an idea, course of action, behavior, or position over a competing set of alternatives. Evidence of acclamation—that is, evidence that has the strong agreement of others—proves these claims. The following are examples of claims of worth:

- Life in preindustrial society was morally superior to life in postindustrial society.
- Standardized testing is superior to course grades in determining student knowledge of a subject area.

Claims of Policy

Claims of policy are statements that set criteria or standards, directly expressing what one ought to do. Evidence of acclamation also supports these statements for taking a specific action or adopting a specific position. The following are examples of claims of policy:

- A policy that penalizes parents of truants by imposing monetary fines should be employed to lessen truancy rates in high schools.
- The best democracy is one that is decentralized and conducts its business locally whenever possible.

As with claims of worth, policy claims demand substantial evidence that demonstrates the course promoted by the stated policy will produce the desired effect stated by the claim.

Claims of Concept

Claims of concept either define or describe a proposition, an idea, or phenomena. These claims are usually definitions justified by expert testimony. The following are examples of claims of concept:

- Emotional intelligence is an individual's interpersonal and intrapersonal competency in dealing effectively with others.
- Groupthink is a blind adherence to the force of will exercised by key members of the group, discounting any opportunity for consideration of dissenting opinion.

Claims of Interpretation

Claims of interpretation provide a frame of reference for understanding an idea. Expert testimony, empirical research, statistical studies, or anecdotal case studies provide the evidence for interpretive claims. Researchers use claims of interpretation to build models, to synthesize data, and to organize factual claims. The following are examples of claims of interpretation:

- Keynesian theory suggests that government economic policy can effectively manage the national economy.
- American Lung Association research concludes that nonsmokers exposed to secondhand smoke at work are at increased risk for adverse health effects.

Figure 2.2	Categories of Claims and Their Uses		
Claim Category	**Type**	**Argument Use**	**Evidence**
Fact	Statements of proposed truth about a person, place, or thing	Propose a claim of fact	Data verifying documentation
Worth	Statements of judgment of the merit of an idea, course of action, behavior, or position	Propose a course of action, behavior, or position	Supportive documentation by experts
Policy	Statements that set criteria or standards	Propose what one ought to do	Supportive documentation by experts or with anecdotal records
Concept	Statements that either define or describe a proposition, idea, or phenomena	Propose definitions	Supportive documentation by experts
Interpretation	Statements that provide a frame of reference for understanding an idea	Propose a framework for combining concepts	Documentation by expert testimony, empirical research, statistical studies, or anecdotal case studies

Source: Toulmin (1999)

A literature review seeks to answer a research question. That question seeks an answer of fact, judgment, standard, definition, or frame of reference. Figure 2.2 synthesizes these classifications. When beginning your literature review, analyze the type of claim needed to answer your research question. Knowing the type of claim needed signals the appropriate evidence and data needed to successfully make the claim.

Claim Acceptability

The reader must have a reason to take a claim as an acceptable assertion, given the question posed. In their 1995 text, *The Craft of Research*, Booth, Colomb, and Williams discuss the four criteria that make strong claims. We have paraphrased those criteria in Figure 2.3.

Figure 2.3	The Four Criteria for an Acceptable Claim	

Criteria		Criteria Characteristic
1	On point	Relates directly to argument.
2	Strong	Gives a compelling reason.
3	Supportable	Evidence is available to justify the position.
4	Understandable	Specific. Clearly stated.

Here is a simple example of a claim that meets the four standards. You are taking a long trip by car, and you notice that you are getting low on gas. You ask yourself, "Should I fill the gas tank now or later?" and you claim, "I should stop at the next gas station and fill up."

This claim is *on point* because it addresses the question posed. It is *strong* because running out of gas would be a major impediment to the trip. The claim is *supportable* because your gas gauge reads nearly empty. Based on your experience, you know you do not have enough gas to reach your destination. Finally, the claim is understandable because it is presented clearly and precisely. You will fill the tank now.

Here is an example of a claim that fails to meet the standards. You are taking a long trip by car, and you notice that you are getting low on gas. You ask yourself, "Should I fill the gas tank now or later?" and you claim, "I should have my oil changed." This claim is not acceptable, because it is not on point (changing the oil fails to address the observation that you are running out of gas). It is not strong (because it does not provide a compelling argument for an oil change). It is not supportable (because the evidence suggests buying gas), and it is not understandable (because there is no clear relationship between the observation and the conclusion).

Here is a thesis that might appear in a literature review: "Student classroom success is directly related to positive classroom social interaction." What would an acceptable claim look like that addresses this thesis? For instance, the following claim could be made: "Individual student classroom success can be directly attributed to a positive interpersonal relationship with the teacher." To decide claim acceptability, apply the four points from Figure 2.3.

1. *Is this claim on point?* Yes, since the claim states that a positive interpersonal relationship with the teacher promotes student achievement, it addresses one aspect of positive classroom social interaction.

2. *Is this claim strong?* Yes, this standard has also been met because the claim provides confirmation of one critical part of classroom interaction, teacher-student relationships, and adds value to the case.

3. *Is this claim supportable?* Yes, there are reasons here that support the claim.

4. *Finally, is this claim understandable?* Assume that key terms and core ideas have been defined. The claim statement specifically defines actor (interpersonal relationship), action (causes), and result (student success). This idea can be clearly observed and analyzed, and thus it is understandable.

CONCEPT 5. BUILDING EVIDENCE

The validity of a claim depends on the evidence provided. Evidence is the second leg of the simple argument (Figure 2.1). As claims drive the argument, so evidence propels the claim. **Evidence** is a set of data presented as the grounds for backing up a claim. One cannot simply assume a claim is true in an argument. Failing to provide supportive evidence, or simply using personal opinion or belief as grounds, renders the claim unfounded, and the persuasive argument fails.

Data Versus Evidence

Data and evidence are not the same. Data are pieces of information. Information is value free and makes no judgment. It simply is. Evidence is data collected for a purpose—data with an agenda. Evidence is the basis for the proof of the claim. How do data become evidence?

To address a claim, a search must be made to seek out relevant data. Once compiled, these data must be arranged in such a manner that the position taken by the claim is supported. Selecting relevant data and compiling them to support the claim transforms data into evidence. Data alone do not signal proof. However, data, when selected and crafted as evidence to support a particular viewpoint, justify a claim. The quality and relevance of the data will control their value as evidence. How data become evidence can be demonstrated by using the rain example presented earlier in this chapter. The forecast is for rain; barometric pressure is steadily falling; cloud formations are building. When taken together, these data become the evidence that rain is likely.

Data Quality

Data quality refers to the strength and credibility of the data as good evidence. High-quality data build strong evidence.

- High-quality data are accurate. They present a true picture of the phenomenon being studied and are an unbiased report of an objective observation.
- High-quality data are precise. They present an exact measurement, description, or depiction of the phenomena.
- High-quality data are authoritative. They are a product of sound research practice.

For example, the following piece of data might be cited as part of a research study:

Study X, an explanatory case study, was conducted in a high-wealth school district with ninth-grade African American students from moderate income to wealthy families. This study sought to explain the reasons for African American student success and failure in algebra classes. The research found that the study population of students failed at the same rate as did their African American counterparts on the national level. It was also found that a positive interaction between the algebra teacher and the student was the major factor attributing to student success. Poverty was not a determining factor for success. Students who did well cited their relationship with their teacher as a major reason for their success, while failing students cited the lack of this relationship as a major reason for their lack of success.

- *Are the data accurate?* You review the study and find that its methods for doing the research were sound. The study was conducted in a rigorous fashion. Its findings were validated. Based on this information, you are satisfied the data are accurate.
- *Are the data precise?* In reviewing the study, you find the interviews with teachers and students followed a strict protocol. The interview questions were structured and were based on well-defined characteristics. Trained interviewers conducted the interviews, and experts outside the study validated the findings. The data were precise.

- *Are the data authoritative?* In reviewing the study's design, method, and procedures, you find the study followed the standards prescribed for case study research. Based on this assessment, you find the data to be authoritative.

Data Relevance

Data must also be relevant. To be relevant, data must meet two standards: Data must be appropriate, and data must be proximate.

Data are *appropriate* when they match the context of the claim. For example, if the claim is making a statement about secondary school teachers' opinions about standardized testing, but the data report the opinions of elementary teachers, then the data are not a match. Elementary teachers are a different population of educators; therefore, their data do not necessarily represent the population that the claim addresses. The data are not relevant.

Data are *proximate* when they provide an accurate account of the phenomena observed. The vantage point or proximity of the observer controls data relevance. The *proximate standard* addresses the accuracy of the data observation. Was the account firsthand or based on secondhand information? Were the data the result of primary research or secondary research that relied heavily on the research of others? Primary data from rigorous research have the best connectivity and are the most convincing.

For example, let us say that a claim makes the statement that more than 75% of elementary school teachers find standardized testing to be of little or no help in planning their curriculum. This claim is based on the results of a national survey of elementary school superintendents (i.e., the data). Because the research did not directly seek elementary school teachers' opinions, the data are not proximate. This research is weak because at best it is a secondhand account. We do not know whether its findings provide a true picture.

Qualifying the Claim

Building a strong claim requires that you present all sides of the debate. Rarely, if ever, is evidence for a claim one-sided. That is, in building evidence to support a claim, you will find data that support your claim and data that oppose your claim. Data that oppose the claim qualify it by either negating or narrowing the claim. Data that narrow the claim either limit the conditions of the claim or the scope of the claim. Data in these instances qualify the claim; they refute or limit the claim. These **qualifiers** demand rebuttal or concession.

An example of negating data could look something like this:

The ABC study showed the target population rating in the 76th percentile in approval of the president's foreign policy. However, when the XYZ study administered a similar questionnaire under the same conditions to the same population, a significant difference was found. Approval had dropped to the 52nd percentile.

The data are contradictory, and their conclusions are in dispute. These studies negate each other.

Narrowing data qualify a claim's assertion. Qualifiers that limit conditions narrow a claim to specific circumstances. In this instance, claims can be narrowed by demographics, age, gender, ethnic background, or locale. Viewpoints such as personal experience, personal beliefs, or professional role can also narrow claims. Here is an example of narrowing data: "When given a survey, executive level managers rated employment compensation as the chief determinant of their job satisfaction. When given the same survey, midlevel managers rated a collaborative work environment as the most significant determinant of job satisfaction." Here the claim asserting a specific reason for job satisfaction presents mixed results. The population surveyed expressed two preferences, compensation and collaborative work environment. The claim must be qualified to assert both viewpoints.

Limiting the scope of the claim narrows the claim's area of assertion. Usually a global assertion claiming a single position of fact is not possible. Claims are always qualified by presenting all sides of the debate.

The literature review builds the case to advocate a thesis position. The case is built on multiple claims supported by acceptable evidence, evidence using relevant and high-quality data. In almost every case, this evidence will present more than one side of the issue. The resulting claims made will set conditions, limits, or boundaries for the thesis, thus qualifying the thesis.

For example, based on the data gathered, the evidence shows that student achievement is mainly the result of positive interaction between students and teachers. However, we also find that factors such as economic background, student and family expectations, academic competency, and peer influences play significant roles in student success. These factors provide limits or boundaries for the thesis and qualify the statement that student achievement is based on positive interaction between the teacher and student.

CONCEPT 6. WARRANT—LOGICALLY CONNECTING THE EVIDENCE TO THE CLAIM

You cannot just present data without organizing them in some reasoned fashion, so the data now become the evidence that logically justifies the claim. Remember, evidence is data with a purpose. The warrant is the connection between the evidence and the conclusion. It is the *because* statement. It is the response to the following sentence: "Based on the evidence presented, the claim made is reasonable and legitimate because. . ."

A warrant frames the evidence by using some rule of logic to draw a reasoned conclusion, thereby justifying the claim. The warrant is the third leg of the simple argument (Figure 2.1).

The term *warrant* takes its definition from early medieval use. As used by monarchs, a king's warrant granted its holder certification to perform certain duties under the authority of the crown. The warrant was a letter of guarantee, a license, and a permit. It allowed the holder safe port and safe passage.

The warrant, as used in the persuasive argument, certifies the argument's safe passage to make its claim. The warrant is the logical license, the rationale that justifies the legitimacy of the evidence as reason to make the claim, making the argument work. Warrants are logical rules of thinking and are seldom stated directly. Remember the example used earlier: "Stop; the light is red." The evidence (the light is red) and claim (stop) are presented here, but the warrant is not. The implied warrant here is the rule—a red signal light means cross traffic has the right of way and we are not allowed to proceed. The statement "The light is red" provides the justification for the claim to stop.

A warrant creates the logical bridge that validates and connects a pattern of evidence in such a way that the reader is persuaded to agree with the conclusion made by the claim. Figure 2.4 illustrates the place of a warrant as the logical bridge in the simple argument.

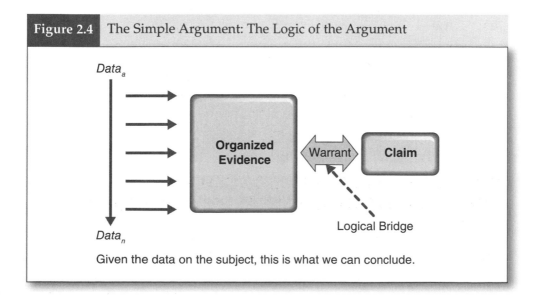

Figure 2.4   The Simple Argument: The Logic of the Argument

Given the data on the subject, this is what we can conclude.

You can discover the warrant of an argument by asking, "What is the reasoning used in this argument that allows me to accept the evidence presented as reasonable proof of the claim?"

For example, a claim is made stating that a well-balanced breakfast should be made available to children in elementary schools. The evidence for this claim comes from many research studies that show children are more attentive and more mentally prepared to begin the school day when they have had a nutritional breakfast. What reasoning is used to justify the claim? In this case, the reasoning used is that the evidence proves the claim beyond a reasonable doubt. If the evidence is sound and it overwhelmingly supports the claim, then you have to agree with the conclusion.

The reasoning behind warrants creates the logic of the argument. Chapter 4 discusses these reasoning patterns and how they are used.

EXERCISE 2.2

Organizing the Argument

Take time now to check your understanding of organizing an argument. We repeat Argument 3 in Exercise 2.1 for you to practice using this tool. Write your answers to the questions below and check your answers with ours that follow.

1. What is the evidence given?

2. What is the stated claim?

3. Review the argument. What is the warrant? What is the reasoning behind the warrant?

Studies X, Y, and Z were used as reasons (evidence) to support the conclusion (claim), "Teamwork is necessary for a long-term work group to be successful in completing the group task." Here are our answers to the questions:

1. The evidence that supports the claim is the various studies cited.

2. The claim is, "Teamwork is necessary for a long-term work group to be successful in completing the group task."

3. The warrant is implied. The implication is that expert evidence is in agreement. Therefore, there is a logical bridge (the warrant) between the evidence and the stated conclusion that teamwork is necessary for group productivity. The logic of the warrant implies that all the evidence points to the same conclusion. Therefore, the conclusion must be correct.

CONCEPT 7. COMPLEX CLAIMS

So far this chapter has dealt with the basics of argumentation using the simple argument. A **simple argument** is a single claim, its evidence, and its warrant. Most arguments are complex. **Complex arguments** are constructed using multiple simple claims. These simple claims serve as the premises of the major argument. A **premise** is a previous statement of fact or assertion (claim) that serves as the evidence for warranting the claim of a major argument. Build complex arguments as follows:

- First, build the simple arguments, using data for each as evidence to justify its claim.
- Then, use the claims produced by these simple arguments as the premises to build the evidence necessary to justify the major claim of the complex argument.

Consider the following example. There are two simple claims: "Young women commit fewer classroom infractions than young men," and "Young women are more adaptable to social situations than are young men." These two claims lead to what we call a **major claim**: "Among all students, male and female, the best-behaved students are female." Notice that these simple claims, when added together, provide the foundation (evidence) for the complex argument and, when taken as fact, lead to a conclusion, the major claim.

A model for the complex argument is seen in Figure 2.5.

Figure 2.5 The Development of the Complex Argument

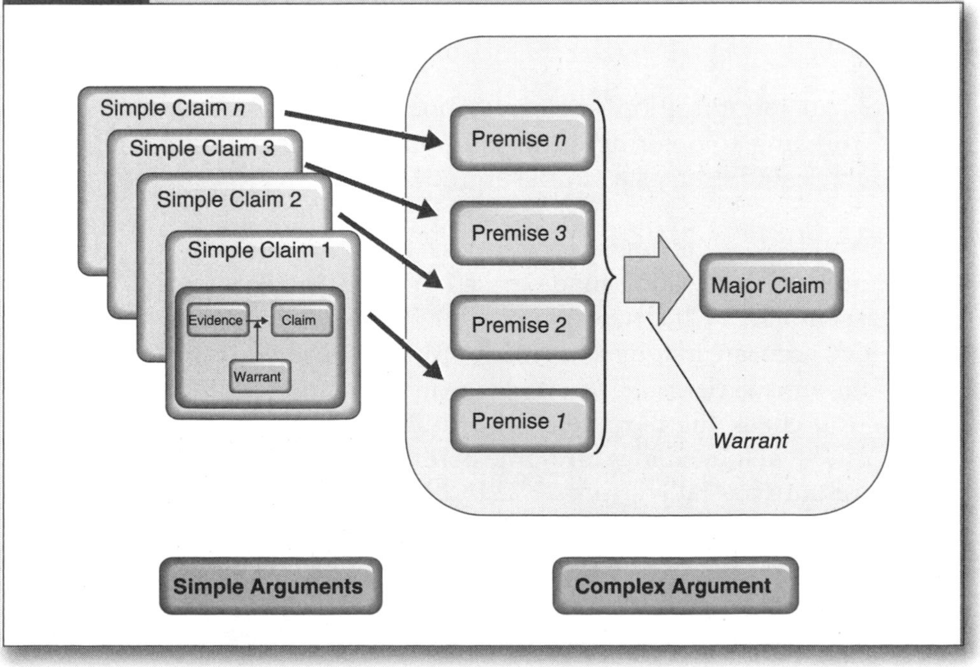

As seen in the figure, simple claims provide the building blocks for the complex argument. Each simple claim becomes a premise of the complex argument. The premises act as the data for the complex argument. When logically organized, they form the evidence for complex claims. The warrants used for justifying the complex arguments can take many acceptable forms and will be explained in depth in Chapters 4 and 5. But, before leaving this topic, let us examine a complex argument in depth.

The rain example presented earlier in Concept 1 is a simple representation of a complex argument. The following analysis shows its simple arguments and how they become the premises to justify the argument's major claim. The example is again presented below.

> Picture an evening in early spring, when changing weather patterns are unpredictable. You are deciding what to wear to work tomorrow. Should you dress for rain? You look at the newspaper and see that the forecast is for rain. You check the barometer and find the pressure steadily falling. You look outside and see that cloud formations are building. You check online and see that storms are predicted for the next few days. When considering all the information gathered, you conclude there is a high likelihood for rain tomorrow. You also decide that the available data indicate the rainstorm will probably hit during your morning commute. You apply the results of this research to your question, "What do I wear to work tomorrow?" and decide to wear a raincoat and take an umbrella.

Problem identification is clear: "Should you dress for rain?" Using critical thinking to determine the solution, relevant data are sought out. Each data point becomes a simple argument.

- "You look at the newspaper and see that the forecast is for rain." The forecast is a claim made based on the meteorological evidence assembled by the newspaper staff. Newspaper forecasts have been 95% accurate in the past, which provides your warrant for accepting this simple claim.
- "You check the barometer and find the pressure steadily falling." You have looked at your home barometer and found that barometric pressure has fallen from 29.72 to 29.45 over the last 6 hours. Because readings like this indicate the pressure drop is rapid, there is a good likelihood that a low-pressure system is approaching, and there is a greater chance of rain.

- "You look outside and see that cloud formations are building." Your observation, that the clouds are thickening rapidly, indicates a good possibility of rain in the near future. You base your conclusion on your prior experience in similar circumstances.
- "You check online and see that storms are predicted for the next few days." You click on the weather app on your tablet. The extended forecast also shows rain approaching. This forecast is based on meteorological evidence supplied from the National Weather Bureau. These forecasts have a 99% accuracy rating and provide the justification accepting this claim.

The four claims, each based on a simple argument, now become the data to form the evidence, the premises, to respond to the question, "What do I wear to work tomorrow?" The conclusion is the major claim, that it would be wise "to wear a raincoat and take an umbrella." The warrant for the conclusion, though unstated, should be obvious. It is an *additive rule of logic*—if all of these things point to the same conclusion, then the legitimacy of its claim is high. We accept the conclusion *because* all of the simple arguments, the premises, point to the same conclusion— dress for rain.

Notice that the two types of arguments presented in Concept 1 are also present here. The four simple claims make up the argument of discovery. Applying the additive rule of logic to these premises, warranting the major claim, the conclusion, makes the advocacy argument. Chapter 4, Surveying the Literature, discusses in detail how a literature survey culminates in the development of the discovery argument. Chapter 5 will explain how the critique of the literature leads to the advocacy argument.

Reading the explanation of the last example might have proved to be a tedious task. The simple fact is that the mental gymnastics of simple claim and complex claim formation are the processes that drive our critical thinking every day. We do hundreds of these gymnastics in the course of our waking hours. We do them without reflection and perhaps at a speed faster than light. They are the mental tools we use to navigate our lives. When formally applied, they become tools to argue a literature review

---

Tips

1. As you progress through your literature review, document the evidence for each claim. This is much easier than going back to search for lost evidence.

2. Check Figure 2.3 often to ensure that your claim types match your argument use and your evidence.

3. Be sure your claims are warranted.

SUMMARY

A successful literature review builds a well-argued case using logically framed arguments. Claims, evidence, and warrants make up logical arguments. A good argument proves its claims. To do this, each claim must be built on credible evidence that validates its assertion. Relevant and credible data provide strong evidence.

Because data provide evidence to justify a claim's assertion, it is your obligation to present all sides of the question. Finally, the warrant supports a claim by using a logical justification to tie the evidence to that claim. Warrants use implied reasoning as justification for a claim.

Simple claims are used as evidentiary building blocks to create complex arguments. These become the premises for justifying the central claim or thesis. Complex arguments are built in two stages. The first stage builds simple claims. The second stage organizes those claims into a body of premises that become the evidence for justifying the complex claim.

At this point you should have a fundamental understanding of the use of argumentation. How is it applied in a literature review? How do you, as the researcher, make use of arguments to survey and critique the literature? What are the strategies for successful argumentation of a case? These topics are addressed in the next three chapters.

CHECKLIST

Task	Completed
Checking Your Simple Argument	
1. Make a list of your simple claims.	☐
2. Check that each claim meets the criteria for acceptability.	☐
3. List the evidence that supports each simple claim.	☐
4. Check how your data are organized as evidence.	☐
5. Are your data strong and credible? Check the standards.	☐
6. Are your data relevant? Again, check the appropriate standards.	☐
7. Properly qualify your data.	☐
8. Warrant each simple argument.	☐
Checking Your Complex Argument	
1. Make a list of your preliminary conclusions.	☐
2. List the premises that support each conclusion.	☐
3. Do the premises justify (warrant) your conclusions?	☐

REFLECTIVE OVERSIGHT

1. Do I really comprehend how the argument of discovery and the argument of advocacy function in building the case for a literature review?

2. Can I define the concept of a basic argument?

3. Do I understand the elements that make up a simple argument?

4. Do I understand the use and validation of the various types of claims?

5. Do I understand the difference between data and evidence and what criteria are required to create strong evidence from data?

6. Do I understand how evidence builds a claim?

7. What creates the logic of the argument?

8. Do I understand how simple claims combine to form complex claims?

9. Is my comprehension of argumentation complete enough to proceed to my next task?

Step 3. Search the Literature

📖 **Task 1.** Select the Literature to Review

📖 **Task 2.** Conduct a Literature Search

　　○ *Activity 1. Manage Your Data*

　　○ *Activity 2. Scan the Literature*

　　○ *Activity 3. Skim the Literature*

　　○ *Activity 4. Map Your Reference Contents*

　　○ *Activity 5. Create Subject Memoranda*

📖 **Task 3.** Refine Your Topic

3

Step Three:
Search the Literature

Search Tasks and Tools

Veni, vidi, vici.

I came, I saw, I conquered.

—Julius Caesar

The Literature Review Model

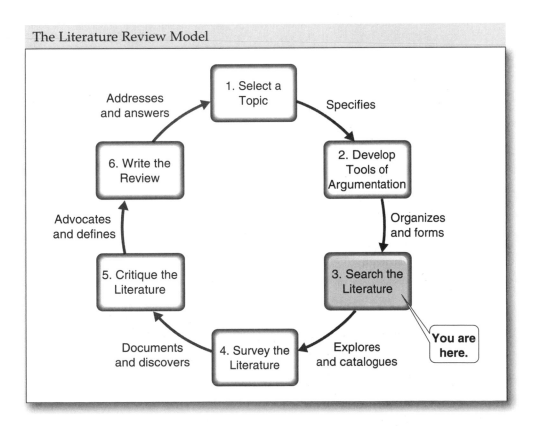

- Addresses and answers
- 1. Select a Topic
- Specifies
- 6. Write the Review
- 2. Develop Tools of Argumentation
- Organizes and forms
- Advocates and defines
- 5. Critique the Literature
- 3. Search the Literature
- You are here.
- Documents and discovers
- 4. Survey the Literature
- Explores and catalogues

KEY VOCABULARY

- **Literature Search**—Collecting, cataloging, and documenting data that will determine salient works and refine the topic.

- **Scanning**—An organized search of library and online catalogs, subject-area encyclopedias, periodical indexes, and abstracts. The scan's purpose is to identify works for possible inclusion in the study.

- **Skimming**—A rapid perusal of possible works to identify important ideas and their specific contribution to the research study and to determine whether or not to use the work.

- **Mapping**—A technique that organizes the results of skimming to put the topic story together, building core idea and author maps and cross-referencing them.

You have successfully completed Step 1 of the literature review: You have defined a research topic. After completing Step 2, you now have a general understanding of the process and tools needed to make an argument. Some researchers make a serious error at this point. They gather the citations from their subject and author queries, go to the stacks, the Internet, and virtual libraries, select books and journals, and begin writing furiously. They fall prey to the misguided notion that now is the time to formally write the review of the literature. But you cannot write what you do not know. So, what's next?

CHAPTER OVERVIEW

At this juncture, a critical-thinking process dictates a deliberate strategy be used to collect and classify information before attempting to build an argument. Writing the literature review, then, requires a plan for assembling and organizing the information gained from the search of the literature. Although it is vital to take notes on your search, there is much examining, analyzing, and synthesizing to do before formal writing can begin. By doing a quality search of the literature, which also means reading and absorbing the information, you will be able to select the literature that needs reviewing. You will probably find, based on this preliminary work in the literature, that your topic can be further refined. Three tasks must be accomplished by the literature search to successfully collect and organize information on your topic. They are (1) selecting literature, (2) doing a **literature search**, and (3) refining your topic. These tasks are the subject of this chapter (Figure 3.1).

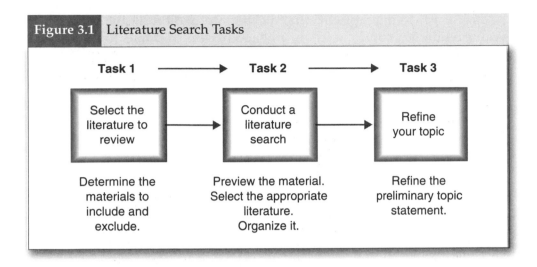

Figure 3.1 Literature Search Tasks

TASK 1. SELECT THE LITERATURE TO REVIEW

At this point in the literature review, select the material to review and the material to be discarded. Several considerations decide what material is suitable for a particular literature search. The main consideration must be finding the information to address the key ideas contained in your preliminary topic statement. Other considerations might apply as well. For example, if the topic is time sensitive, look carefully at dates of publication. A 1940s text is probably no help if the topic title begins, "Latest Theories on...." But perhaps your topic involves synthesizing the major works addressing a subject. If so, search for the important authors and theories about the topic, regardless of date. The topic statement provides the direction and boundaries of your search. Using the topic statement as a pathfinder, continually ask yourself the following two questions:

1. What is the subject of my inquiry?

2. What literature must I include that will tell me about the subject?

After selecting the literature to review, a second and equally important task should also take place: beginning to refine your preliminary topic. The topic is fluid and subject to change at this stage in the literature review because knowledge of any literature does not yet influence your topic understanding. The data gathered while completing a search of the literature will impact your topic knowledge. The literature selected from the search will qualify and refine the topic statement, causing it to narrow and become more concrete. As the research continues, reflect on how the relevant literature you gather influences and molds the topic. For example, you may discover that the preliminary topic is too broad and that it would be unrealistic to attempt covering all the information on the subject. Or, your preliminary topic choice may be too narrow and fails to address the substantial information necessary to answer the thesis question.

Next, examine and reflect on the impact of the search data on your topic understanding. These deliberations should help you further develop a topic statement. Be aware of the influence the literature has on the conduct of the search. Be mindful and deliberate while conducting the search. Keep these three questions in mind when reflecting on your topic:

1. What is the literature telling me about my topic?

2. How is my understanding of my research topic changing?

3. What should my topic statement be now?

TASK 2. CONDUCT A LITERATURE SEARCH

The second task of Step 3 requires collecting and selecting data. This task requires completing three separate activities: (1) previewing the material, (2) selecting the appropriate literature, and (3) organizing the chosen literature (Figure 3.2).

Figure 3.2	Literature Search Tasks and Tools

Search Task	Search Tools
Literature Preview	Scan
Content Selection	Skim
Data Organization	Map

Three tools will help you complete this task. These tools are (1) **scanning** the literature, (2) **skimming** potential works for content, and (3) **mapping** the suitable works for inclusion in the study. While these are three separate techniques, you may use them in various ways depending on your ability and your topic selection.

Think of searching the literature as assembling a well-used jigsaw puzzle. There are always parts missing, and often pieces of other puzzles have become intermixed. Developing a strategy for assembling a jigsaw puzzle is simple: Find a table with room to spread out the puzzle. Ensure that you have enough room to sort pieces and to organize them. Make sure there is good lighting. Consider what the puzzle should look like when completed by looking at the picture on the box. Spread the puzzle pieces out on the table. Look for pieces that obviously do not belong and set them aside. Look for the puzzle pieces that make up the outer edges. Assemble them and sort the remaining pieces by like pattern. Look for matching color patterns and notice the specific shape of each piece. Finally, put the puzzle together one piece at a time.

Assembling a jigsaw puzzle is similar to searching the literature. Open the box and spread the puzzle pieces on the table by consulting subject and author indices for potential texts and materials for possible review. The key terms and core ideas of the preliminary topic statement define the search. They represent the boundaries of your research puzzle. Scan the library materials, reflecting on pieces that are part of the research puzzle. Keep in mind that some puzzle pieces are not part of this jigsaw puzzle. Remove these first. Then begin collecting the pieces of this puzzle. Catalog the remaining materials found to make them available for the next stage of the search, skimming.

Skimming resembles a second sorting of the jigsaw puzzle pieces. As with the jigsaw puzzle, data gathered from the scan of the literature will be studied for usefulness. What should you include? What parts should you discard? Skim the materials collected in the scan to decide their individual appropriateness for inclusion in the study. What part of this work addresses the topic? In what way? The preliminary topic statement provides the frame for deciding what to include. After deciding what will be useful in the study, address the final task of the search, mapping.

As with the jigsaw puzzle, examine the remaining materials to determine their potential place in the literature review. How do these data explain a core idea? How do these data further define the key words of the topic statement? Organize the literature review puzzle by documenting the place each of the selected materials has in developing the topic statement. After completing the literature search, organize the information for inclusion in the review. Weed out data that do not directly address the topic and then organize the remaining material by key idea, noting the specific contribution that each piece will make when explaining the topic. Remember the two questions that guide your literature search:

1. What is the subject of my inquiry?

2. What literature must I include that will tell me about the subject?

Activity 1. Managing Your Data

Before beginning your search, you must decide how to catalog and document the information pertaining to the topic. Be aware that without careful management, data can overwhelm you. At this point in the literature search, you only need to log two types of information, bibliographic information and scan progress.

Bibliographic Documentation

Bibliographic documentation for an entry includes author, title, data, publisher, ISBN or ISSN number, pages referenced, and the call number. The advances in digitization of online resources have required new cataloging protocols. Data collection online must be appropriately cited. URLs (uniform resource locators) are used to reference information collected via Web browser or other types of Internet software. DOIs (digital object identifiers) are used when citing information obtained from digital networks providing citation-linking services, such as CrossRef. List each entry by idea or descriptor. These identifiers will become the initial search terms used when conducting the literature search.

Using the old standby 3x5 card stack or building a digital card stack is the simplest method for documenting and cataloging information. However, we recommend you use integrated cataloging and documentation software, introduced in Chapter 1, such as EndNote, Citation, or RefWorks, which are available online or at college bookstores. RefWorks is a Web-based bibliographic database manager. It is available at no cost from most university libraries. Similar to EndNote and Citation, RefWorks allows you to create a personal database and bibliographies tailored to your topic. It also allows you to import documents from most of the online databases directly into its database. RefWorks will automatically format your references in most academic styles, such as MLA or APA. EndNote and Citation will do the same and offer additional cataloging and documentation enhancements as well.

Using software simplifies the process and allows you to integrate information as you go along. Basic bibliographic information serves as the reference point for succeeding search tasks. Documentation and cataloging are cumulative. Each new search increases the information you have gathered. Use a bibliographic entry card, such as that shown in Figure 3.3, or the appropriate software data entry page to document your data.

By employing the techniques and tools presented in this section, you can now perform the following:

- Successfully develop a specific scanning strategy that connects the preliminary topic statement, its focus, and its perspective to key ideas.
- Frame key ideas as descriptors for the search.
- Develop cataloging tools to document the works you plan to review for potential inclusion in the study.
- Define the sequence and purpose for each scan and identify appropriate search databases and their accessibility.

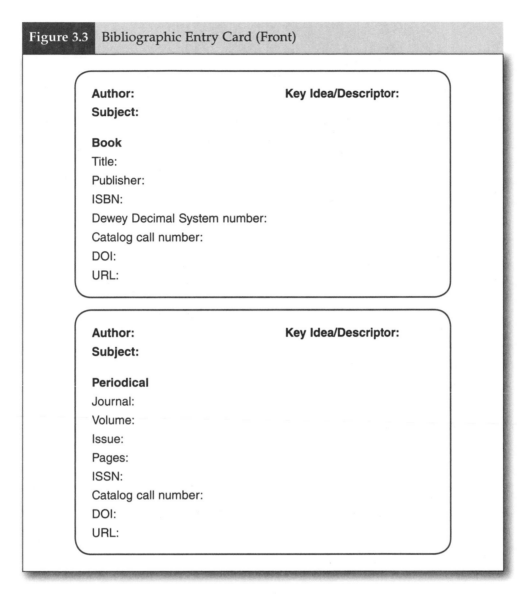

Figure 3.3   Bibliographic Entry Card (Front)

Activity 2. Scanning the Literature

A literature scan is a systematic canvassing of library and online catalogs, subject-area encyclopedias, periodical indexes, and abstracts. The scan's purpose is to identify potentially useful works, which could be books, articles, theses, dissertations, reports, and conference proceedings. When scanning, quickly examine each of the reference catalogs or guides, identifying the works you might want to include. You will typically engage in multiple scanning sessions, each designed to cover a particular view or subject of the study. Each scan carefully identifies literature references based on their usefulness in building the topic's case. Design the scans to seek out various types of topic content, theoretical foundations and definitions, discussion and debate, current issues, field problems, and functional applications. Literature sources are usually categorized by these content types and are in chronological order of publication. You can place content types in a sequence based on specific content, publication type, and publication time frame (Figure 3.4).

Different literature sources contain different categories of information. You would not look at trade magazines to search for the theoretical foundations of a topic, nor would you search definitive texts for recent issues or practices. The strategy for each scanning session should consider the information category needed and the suitable research database that contains that literature type.

Figure 3.4	Literature References				
Recency	*Years*	*Months*	*Weeks*	*Days*	*Current*
Resource Type	Books, monographs, dissertations, and reference works	Journals and periodicals	Popular and trade magazines	Newspapers	Websites and blogs
Content Type	Theoretical foundations, definitions, research, key concepts, and constructs	Recent research, theoretical discussion, and debate	Current issues, debates, applications, practices, and field problems	Current issues, debates, and field problems	Up-to-date issues, debates, practices, and applications

An academic literature review for practitioners most often demands that you seek both theoretical and field-based knowledge. Use current field-based literature to decide the issues, significance, and relevance of the study. The theoretical literature clearly defines the topic and provides the knowledge base for understanding the topic's depth and breadth. A search for the most recent data (see Figure 3.4) can help you gather information dealing with topic significance and relevance to a particular academic body of knowledge or professional practice. Specific databases contain different literature types. Figure 3.5 provides a categorical listing of databases by literature type. For an up-to-date listing of databases that directly address the specific academic discipline of the study, confer with a research librarian or consult the library's online database directory.

Begin the scan by doing a query of the reference databases that match the focus, vantage point, and content of the literature you are studying. For example, let's assume that you have identified your research interest as theories of intelligence and that your selected vantage point is cognitive psychology. You might begin the search by querying online using Google Scholar. Using the keywords "intelligence theory" would produce hundreds of references. To filter out irrelevant sites, refer to your preliminary topic statement and the information generated from the subject-area encyclopedia and handbook queries. Quickly peruse the remaining items noting titles, authors, publication names, and dates of publication, as appropriate. The resulting information will provide an initial overview of the authors and texts that can be used in the literature search. You might even explore the most relevant citations to gather additional search data. Search engines such as Google Scholar provide listings for books, articles, dictionaries and more. You will have a wide range of potential research materials. To navigate this resource efficiently, use the qualifiers, preliminary topic statement, and reference definitions as guides to find the relevant information about your topic. Do not select citations to review by relying on what shows up first on the Web page.

This work will provide a starting point that might well lead to searches of each research database type as listed in Figure 3.5. Search directories are databases that use a query to obtain information. The most common query uses Boolean logic to frame the database search. A *Boolean search* uses keywords connected by the logical operators *and, or,* and *not* to define the search of the database. Using a combination of keywords and one or more of the Boolean operators, you can focus the query and narrow the search to a specific area of interest.

| Figure 3.5 | Reference Databases |

Literature type	Database
Books, subjects, authors	• Library catalogs • Online public access catalogs
Refereed journals, subject periodicals	• Library based and online subject indices and abstracts
Theses and dissertations	• Dissertation abstracts
Trade magazines, popular magazines, newspapers	• Online indices • Web query
Websites and blogs	• Online search engines and databases

Here is how it works. Select a key idea from your preliminary topic statement and break it down by its key terms. Using the key terms as descriptors, combine the descriptors with the Boolean operators (*and, or, not*) to frame the search question. Use the operator *and* between two key terms to narrow the search selection. For example, say you are conducting a search about the key idea, "What is the nature of human intelligence?" Using three key terms—*theories, human,* and *intelligence*—a Boolean search might be "theories and human and intelligence." Notice that you can narrow the query by linking the two descriptors together to match the key idea. You can also narrow the search by author and subject: "Gardner and Wexler and Terman and intelligence." In this case, you are designing a query to find what these three theorists have to say about intelligence.

The Boolean operator *not* excludes terms from the search. Again using the previous key idea on theories of intelligence, you would query the database as follows: "theories and intelligence not emotional." This query will search for theories of intelligence and exclude any works that reference the word *emotional* in the text. When possible, avoid using the operator *not* because it tends to exclude documents you could actually use.

Using the Boolean operator *or* expands or broadens the query. The principal use here is to include similar ideas. For example, suppose you are exploring the key idea of the cultural bias of standardized tests. Frame the query in the following manner: "cultural bias and standardized tests or assessments or testing." Here you expand the query to include more descriptors that could well provide important banks of information about the key idea. Mix and match the Boolean operators to best fit the key idea of the search. You may need to use a trial-and-error method of framing the descriptors and operators into a statement in order to produce the needed result. Figure 3.6 summarizes the use of Boolean operators.

Figure 3.6	Boolean Operators	
Operator	**Topic search**	**Descriptor use**
and	Narrows	Links descriptors
not	Excludes	Qualifies descriptors
or	Broadens	Adds descriptors

Use the Internet and Your University's Virtual Library

You will probably be using the Internet for data gathering as part of your literature search. The Internet has quickly become a necessary storehouse for information and is, in fact, a library. The Internet supplies information from seemingly infinite sources. Be careful, though. Internet data sources vary in their credibility, accuracy, and soundness. Two major problems with the Internet are that it has neither quality control nor a librarian. In your university library, whether it is a bricks-and-mortar structure or a virtual library, a research librarian can help you find the data you need and provide expertise in judging the quality of the material you seek.

On the Internet, you must be your own librarian. You must judge data quality, authority, and applicability. Remember, anybody can put inaccurate information online. You want to quote only from scholarly sources, experts in the field, but such papers will be mixed in with nonscholarly works. Take extra pains to ensure that data you find on the Internet are high quality, authentic, and correctly cited.

We recommend that you use the online databases provided through your academic institution on your university's library Web page. University libraries have developed a comprehensive virtual collection of databases that mirror, and in many cases extend, available library resources. These databases have been checked by librarians and are at your disposal for doing research. The library research staff can coach you through the use and applicability of the electronic references. These references can include online connectivity to virtual research librarians, access to the major journals and reports for your field of study, virtual texts, connectivity to university library networks, and many other services. A typical university library Web page provides a search function to query by author, title, or keyword. This search will produce a list of the texts, journals, dissertations, and relevant research projects available in your library, listing both electronic and hard copy materials. Again, using your preliminary topic statement as a guide, sort through the data for the relevant materials on your topic.

Additionally, databases such as EBSCO, GALE, JSTOR, ProQuest, and SAGE e-reference are excellent search destinations. Each of these databases ties to particular academic fields. For additional help, use Thomas Mann's excellent text, *The Oxford Guide to Library Research*. This is a seminal work that provides in-depth library research assistance on any topic. Figure 3.7 is a chart listing the most popular academic databases and their holdings.

Since you know the perspective and the unit of analysis for your study, you know your academic field. Using this information makes it easy to select the appropriate databases to query. Online public access catalogs (OPACs), the text catalogs for your university stacks, or Link +, the catalog of texts available to you from other university libraries, provide excellent sources for your text search. The use of online academic databases, such as WORLDCAT, GALE and EBSCO, will also provide fruitful results.

Figure 3.7	Online Academic Databases

Online Academic Databases	Contents
EBSCO	Using several research databases, e-books, and e-journals, EBSCO provides an information service that covers several different subject areas in the social sciences.
GALE	GALE offers a virtual reference library of encyclopedias, e-books, and monographs in its Gale Virtual Reference Library. GALE Infotrac provides full indexing and text export for periodicals across multiple disciplines.
JSTOR	JSTOR is a digital library containing academic journals, books, and primary sources in both digital and print formats in the areas of social science, literature, education, the fine arts, mathematics, and science.
PROQUEST	ProQuest is a collection of databases covering international literature in social sciences, providing an index and full text for articles from over 1,000 social science journals.
SAGE PREMIER	SAGE is a database providing access to over 650 peer-reviewed full text journals published by SAGE in the multiple academic disciplines including social science and humanities.
WORLDCAT/ FIRSTSEARCH	WORLDCAT is a central indexing system that includes 2,000 e-content collections containing articles, e-books, and other contents from databases, including EBSCO, GALE, and PROQUEST, linking over 1 billion electronic, digital, and physical resources from libraries worldwide.

As you prepare to do the literature search, consult with your research librarian for coaching on the use of the electronic resources your university provides and which resources will provide the best fit for your search.

One note of caution before leaving this topic: Many of the journals provided through university electronic databases connect directly with personal research databases, such as EndNote, Citation, and RefWorks. This means that you can cite a journal, transfer its abstract, and catalog its contents with one click of a mouse. The good news is that you can document and catalog this information quickly. The bad news is that little, if any, of this knowledge transfers to your consciousness. Make use of the great improvements electronic databases provide to the task of searching, but take the time to understand and internalize the meaning of your information as you collect the data. Keep written notes and **memoranda** on your research, including online research.

EXERCISE 3.1

Beginning Your Search

Check your understanding about literature searching by applying what you have learned to your own project.

1. Write your topic, as you currently understand it.

2. List the literature types that address the core ideas of your topic (see Figure 3.4).

3. List the databases you plan to use for your first scan of the literature (see Figure 3.5).

Scan Progress

Keep a log of the material that scanning has determined may be useful for inclusion in your research. Logging can be done in two ways. First, you can work directly from your Boolean query lists. As you scan, cross out items that will be excluded from your study. Those items that remain on the list will be used in the next stage of your research work. This procedure ensures that you do not miss any potential resources. The second method uses a database documentation program, such as EndNote, rather than using the hard copy generated in the first method. You can winnow the data using the tools within the software.

Activity 3. Skimming the Literature

The next job is to skim the identified works to decide what materials will be useful. Skimming quickly identifies the important ideas contained in a text. While scanning identifies potential information to include in your study, skimming selects the best of all potential information. Here, you decide what to include and what to omit. Two standards guide you in conducting the literature skim:

1. Will this work be included or excluded from the study?

2. If included, what in this work is useful?

Use two techniques when skimming. First, examine and review the table of contents or index to locate specific material applicable to your topic. Second, do a quick read of those sections, chapters, or subchapters to decide whether (and if so, where) that information fits with the topic statement. Skimming identifies, organizes, and catalogs the specific material for review. Document the skimming results on the back of the bibliographic entry card or on your electronic data entry page. Figure 3.8 is an example of how this might look.

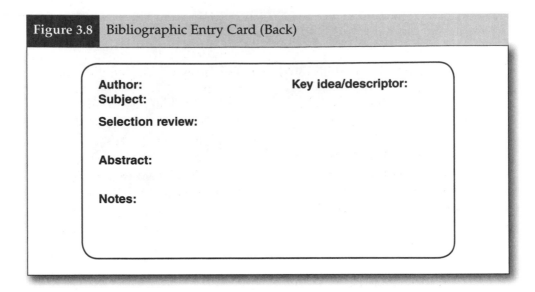

Figure 3.8   Bibliographic Entry Card (Back)

> **Author:**   **Key idea/descriptor:**
> **Subject:**
> **Selection review:**
>
> **Abstract:**
>
> **Notes:**

1. Begin skimming by reviewing the abstract or the text's introduction.

2. Does this material address the topic statement of the literature review? If so, how?

3. Continue by examining the table of contents of the text or major subject headings of the periodical. Note those chapters or sections that address the key terms or core ideas in the topic statement of the literature review.

4. Document the results in the selection review section of the bibliographic entry card. Make sure that each entry documents the specific ideas and identifies the document, including the page numbers that you plan to use.

5. Once you have selected the specific areas of the text or periodical, do a quick read of that section to find the relevant information. Conduct a quick read by reading the first (introduction) and the last (conclusion) paragraphs of the section to identify the main ideas.

6. Read the section at three to four times your normal rate to quickly gather the main ideas.

7. Note the main ideas in the abstract section of the bibliographic entry card. Again, be sure to include page references for each major idea.

8. Be sure to check all glossaries, appendixes, and other information in the end matter of the book. If there is a glossary, skim it for definitions connected to the topic's core ideas or key terms. Document these as well.

To continue the earlier example, suppose the research topic is, "What is the nature of individual human intelligence?" The results of the literature scan identified several potential sources, which you have cataloged. You are ready to skim. One of the texts cited is *Intelligence Reframed,* by Howard Gardner. After reading the introduction, you decide this text will make a major contribution to your literature review. In reviewing the table of contents, you find the first seven chapters deal directly with your core idea, psychological theories of intelligences, so you note each chapter title and page number in the selective review section on the bibliographic entry card. You then read the opening and closing paragraphs and skim the body of each chapter. You document the main ideas of each chapter in the abstract section of the bibliographic entry card. In the notes section of the bibliographic entry card, you also document Appendix D of the text, which contains the contact list for theorists in multiple intelligence theory. Next, proceed to use this skimming technique for each of the texts selected.

Activity 4. Mapping Your Materials

Once skimming is completed, begin mapping to form the data's patterns. Mapping is a technique for organizing the works to be included in the literature review. Analyze each selected work for its contribution to the topic statement. Remember, the topic statement consists of core ideas and key terms. These ideas and terms are the descriptors on the bibliographic entry card. The content relevant to the descriptors should be noted and cataloged. In this phase of the search, you discover where each piece of the material gathered fits in with understanding the topic. Mapping allows you to organize the data collected into a pattern from which analysis can emerge.

Use the descriptors created when you developed the preliminary topic statement as the central themes of your content maps. You might also create maps that use the key terms and descriptors as major headings to map the data. Either of these methods can be equally useful for patterning information. Here you can effectively employ your personal research database software. Query by key terms or by authors. The relevant sites will be listed, providing the material for the map.

Map during the literature search to picture how material collected from the scan and skim addresses the topic statement. Then, develop content and author maps to pattern the information. Map the literature as follows:

1. Use your literature search key descriptors as central themes to create core idea maps. Map the data by each theme.

2. Compare your topic statement to the core maps to ensure the completeness of the information gathered by the scan and skim of the literature. If you find gaps or omissions, scan and skim the literature again.

3. Reorganize the data by author to document theory knowledge and citations. Expand the data detail when creating author maps.

4. Review the maps. Now that you have a general idea about the basic information addressing your topic, do you need to revise your topic statement? If so, rewrite the topic statement to reflect your new topic understanding.

Mapping by Core Idea

A core idea map isolates each of the core ideas of the preliminary topic as a central idea. These maps answer the question, "What is known about this subject?"

Figure 3.9   Core Idea Map

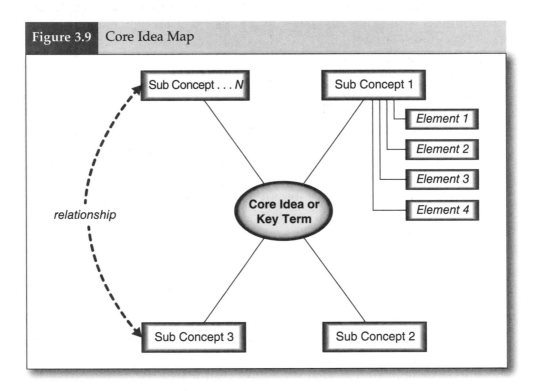

Review the model in Figure 3.9. Notice the core idea, or descriptor, is in the center and serves as the central idea or theme of the map. Each of the categories or parts that make up the core idea should be sketched as a subsidiary, or supporting, idea. These parts can be different theoretical positions, or they can be definitional or descriptive categories. Various arrangements are possible, such as type, theme, or chronology, depending on what makes the most sense given the particular research question. Break down each of the subsidiary ideas into individual categories, such as research studies, theories, definitions, or examples. You may also further break down individual parts. How you depict each of these maps will depend on the core idea and the parts that define it. The key to the successful development of a core idea map is the story it tells. As you develop the map, consider the following questions:

1. Is the depiction clear, inclusive, and comprehensive?

2. Does the map document the current state of knowledge about the core idea?

Complete a core idea map for each of the ideas, key descriptors, or key terms outlined in your first subject map. One last word about core mapping: Use this tool continually as you complete the remaining steps of the literature review. Core maps help navigate, survey, and analyze the literature. They serve as guideposts in refining the research topic. Finally, they are excellent reference tools for developing the composition outline of the literature review document.

Figure 3.10 (see page 76) is an example of a beginning core map on the history of the theory of human intelligence. The key descriptor, the main map topic, for this map is "The history of the Theory of Intelligence." Five themes were produced to address this descriptor, beginning with "Intelligence as an Abstraction." Notice that themes are arranged chronologically to show the evolution of studying intelligence theory. Each theme is further explained by subsidiary ideas—subtopics—that pattern the data gathered by scanning and skimming. Each subtopic has author references to cross-reference the information.

Mapping by Author Contribution

The author map documents the literature review differently. It depicts the material assembled from the scan and skim of the literature from the vantage point of an authority. While the core idea map organized the material based on subject knowledge, the author map organizes the material by individual contributor. The core idea map answers the question, "What is known about this subject?" The author map responds to the question, "Who said it?" Figure 3.11 (see page 77) shows an example of an author map.

Author mapping provides depth and reference specificity to support core idea mapping. When author mapping, develop maps depicting the work of each author cited in the literature review and cross-reference this information to a core idea map.

1. Note each specific text. Obtain this information from the author and selection review sections of the bibliographic entry card.

2. Record on your map the relevant ideas and details from the text, organizing them by content, theory explanation, or chapter headings and subheadings. This information is in the abstract and notes sections of the bibliographic entry card or the software data entry page.

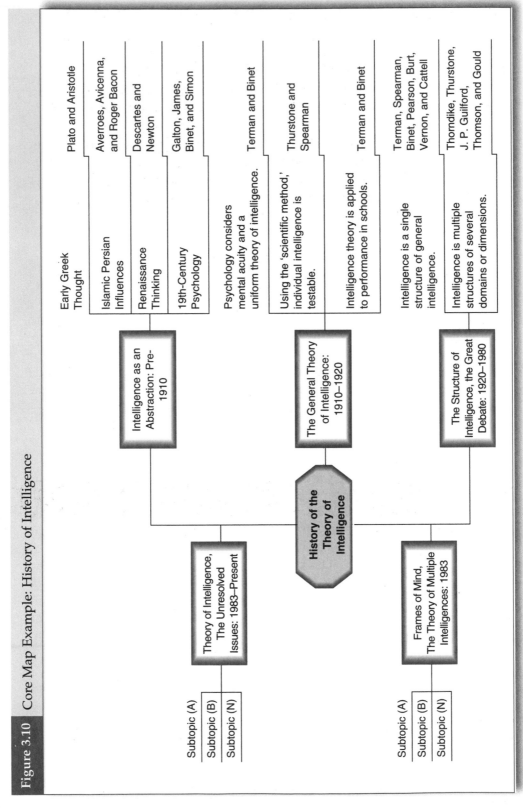

Figure 3.10   Core Map Example: History of Intelligence

3. Record the relationships among the texts depicted on the author map. These connections compare theories, cross-reference subject information, and develop chronological connections among texts. Place more information on these author maps, including page number references, notable quotes, and other authors or texts cited. As with the scanning and skimming techniques, adapt mapping skills and designs to your preferences and needs.

Figure 3.11   Author Map

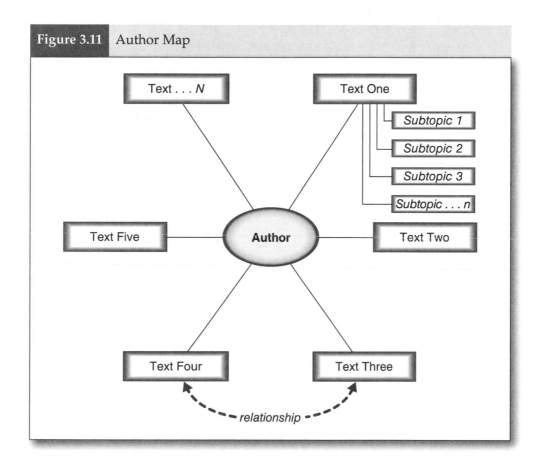

Activity 5. Creating Subject Memoranda

Now is the time to create notes on what you have learned about your topic. After studying your maps, write up what you have seen. This is also the time to develop preliminary ideas. Reread what you have written and edit it as necessary. Next, use your memoranda to organize your thoughts from mapping.

If you have difficulty completing this exercise, review this chapter. If you are able to complete this exercise successfully, continue entering other references into your management tool.

EXERCISE 3.2

Practicing Doing a Literature Search

Practice what you have learned so far. Use the list you created in Exercise 3.1 to complete this exercise.

1. Which method—3x5 card, Citation, Endnotes, or RefWorks—will you use for cataloging your data?

2. Enter the core ideas from your topic statement into your selected management tool.

3. Prepare your management tool for data entry.

4. Scan your references and select one reference to work on.

5. Skim the selected reference for appropriate data to include in your review.

6. Enter the selected data into your management tool.

7. Develop a suitable core idea map.

8. Build a cross-referenced author map.

9. Write and edit subject memoranda for your search.

TASK 3. REFINE YOUR TOPIC

Remember, the topic statement defines what is to be learned. It also forms the boundary of the study. This is an important notion. Not long ago we asked a colleague, a researcher from the University of Chicago, how he approached studying a topic. His answer surprised us: "For me, I spend less time thinking about what I am trying to study. Where I spend my time is in the hard thinking about what I am not going to study." The boundaries provided by the topic statement define the study from two perspectives, that which is to be studied and that which is not to be studied. This "hard thinking," deciding what is not to be studied, allows you to build a framed and focused topic of a study. How much is enough, and whether you have enough, are the wrong questions to ask. The questions you should ask at this stage are as follows:

1. Do I have a clear understanding of the core ideas in my topic statement?

2. Are these core ideas backed up adequately by my literature search?

3. Based on the literature search, how has my topic statement changed?

4. In reviewing my core idea and author maps, have I chosen too broad or too narrow a topic?

Completing a literature search is a great opportunity to refine the preliminary topic statement. You have examined and defined the core ideas and key terms, and you know their main ideas. You may now revise the focus and vantage point taken in your topic statement for accuracy and clarity based on the information produced by the literature search. Now explore whether the topic is too broad. Do the author maps contain hundreds of citations, and could each individual core idea map be a study in itself? What to do? The simple answer is to reframe the research topic statement by narrowing the focus. For example, your topic may be, "What are the negative connections that exist among members of a group?" When scanning the literature, you find an overwhelming quantity of data addressing this topic, so you decide to narrow the focus. Your strongest interest is in the connections built among individuals in work groups. Refine the topic to now state, "What negative connections can exist in work group dyads?"

Limiting the core ideas and the specific theory areas of study, or narrowing the subject of study, are ways to refine the vantage point. You might further qualify your interest by selecting a specific vantage point. For example, your original study focus might have been group psychology and psychodynamics. You now refine your topic statement to ask, "What are the psychodynamics present in negative relationships of dyads in work groups?" By limiting the focus to a subset (dyads in work groups) of the larger category (groups) and by specifying a specific discipline to study (psychodynamics), the topic area contracts to a workable dimension.

You can further define the subject demographically. You can delimit the topic statement by gender, age, experience, geographical location, ethnic background, or other qualification. In addition, you can further narrow the previous topic example by asking, "What are the psychodynamics present in negative relationships of dyads comprising adult males in work groups with a membership of fewer than fifteen?"

There are many ways to narrow a topic of study. Ask yourself the following two questions when trying to narrow the topic:

1. What am I actually trying to study?

2. What am I not going to study?

As a guide to narrowing the topic, refer to the research interest statement used to define the topic. Refer also to your work in Exercise 1.6, Refining Your Research Topic Statement, to further edit the research topic statement. The results of your literature search may have produced scant information on the topic. In this case, you should review the key terms and core ideas developed in building your topic.

1. Have you defined your key terms and core ideas correctly?

2. Are there other definitions and academic vantage points that could produce better results?

3. Should the research become more inclusive by expanding either the focus or vantage point selected?

Examining the omissions and weaknesses that the literature search reveals is also a good way to expand the topic statement. When either narrowing or broadening the topic statement, keep in mind that quality is the critical standard of a research project. Narrowing or broadening the topic statement is not about how much work you need to do, but what work you must do to address the research topic.

Tips

1. Be diligent. Slow down. Completing the many tasks necessary for a high-quality literature search may seem time consuming. It is. However, the various tasks you perform correctly now will save time in the future. Careful, accurate research done once is much more efficient than hurried research that must be repeated again and again.

2. Organize. Careful organization of information at the beginning will save you from the daunting task of trying to organize at the end when there is far too much material.

SUMMARY

You now have a way to assemble the puzzle. You know that a literature search is strategic data collection. It involves the three tasks of selecting possible material, searching the material for inclusions, and refining the topic statement. Three tools are available to help in conducting the search—scanning, skimming, and mapping. Keeping journals and memoranda is also useful for organizing and remembering the increasing amount of information. Memoranda are particularly useful for refining a topic statement.

Use the information you now have to analyze the breadth and depth of your topic. After the search, you can select the works to include for review and, with careful reflection, further define and refine the topic of study.

CHECKLIST

Task	Completed

Previewing the Data

1. Conduct scans of potential works by topic ideas and key terms. ☐

2. Conduct scans of potential works to build the case for study significance and relevance. ☐

Managing the Data

1. Catalog bibliographic information. ☐

2. Create an historical log of the scan process. ☐

3. Create a database structure. ☐

Reviewing the Data

1. Examine the major parts of potential works for inclusion. ☐

2. Quickly read selected work for pertinent data. ☐

Mapping the Data

1. Build initial core maps by core ideas and key terms. ☐

2. Build maps by major contributing author. ☐

Refining Your Research Topic

1. Refine topic statement for accuracy and clarity. ☐

2. Revise topic statement as necessary. ☐

REFLECTIVE OVERSIGHT

1. Am I satisfied with my scanning? What else do I need to know to find potential works for my study?

2. Have I created a usable database structure?

3. Am I satisfied with my selection of potential works for inclusion in my study? If not, what skills and knowledge do I need to complete this task?

4. Have I successfully been able to map my data? If not, what else do I need to do?

5. Do I have a researchable topic?

Step 4. Survey the Literature

- 📖 **Task 1.** Assemble the Collected Data
  - ○ *Activity 1. Catalog the Data*

- 📖 **Task 2.** Organize the Information
  - ○ *Activity 1. Arrange Information to Build Evidence*
  - ○ *Activity 2. Organize the Information and Build Claims*

- 📖 **Task 3.** Analyze the Patterns of Data
  - ○ *Activity 1. Map the Discovery Argument*
  - ○ *Activity 2. Analyze the Argument*

4

Step Four:
Survey the Literature

Building the Argument of Discovery

Cui cerca, trova; cui secuta, vinci.

One who seeks, finds; one who perseveres, wins.

The Literature Review Model

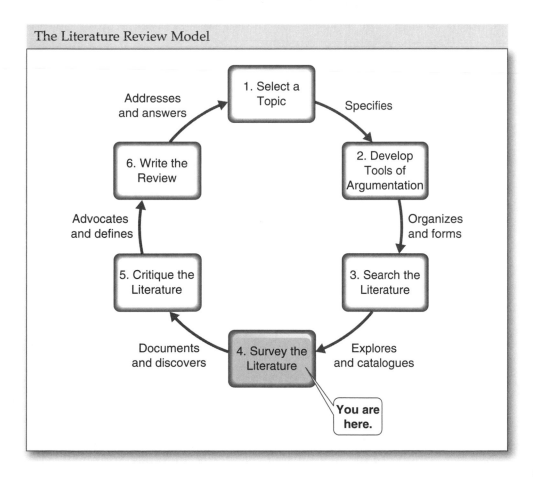

<table>
<tr><td colspan="1">

KEY VOCABULARY

- **Argument of Advocacy**—An argument based on claims that have been proven as fact and which serve as the premises for logically driving a conclusion—in this case, the thesis statement of the literature review.

- **Argument of Discovery**—An argument proving that the findings of fact represent the current state of knowledge regarding the research topic.

- **Evidence**—A set of data presented as the grounds for substantiating a claim.

- **Reasoning**—To discover, formulate, and conclude by the use of a carefully conducted analysis.

</td></tr>
</table>

A good literature review must build a case based on evidence to prove the research thesis. Remember from Chapter 2 that findings and conclusions are made by presenting two arguments—the discovery argument and the advocacy argument. The discovery argument presents the findings or evidence that answer the question, "What do we know about the subject of our study?" The advocacy argument answers the question, "Based on what we know, what conclusions can be drawn as a response to the research question?" At this point, you may be saying, "Okay, I get what these arguments are and what they do, but how do I make them?"

CHAPTER OVERVIEW

This question is easily answered if we apply critical thinking to the process of doing a literature review. Critical thinking requires collecting and compiling all pertinent data first. This is done to ensure that the appropriate information is available before attempting to develop findings. Once data are gathered, you can sift through that information to *discover the evidence and build the argument* to answer, "What do we know?" about the issue in question. After you have made the discovery argument, this evidence can be applied to draw the necessary conclusions to answer the initial question or solve the problem. We can make the statement, "Based on what we know, this is what we can conclude . . . ."

The literature review process follows the same path. Step 3, search the literature, requires collecting the pertinent data about the research topic. Step 4, survey of the literature, then, develops the evidence and argument using the data collected from Step 3 to answer the question, "What is known about the topic?" The critique of the literature, Step 5, asks, "Based on what we know, what conclusions can be drawn to answer the research question?" Simply put, the survey of the literature develops the discovery argument, while the critique of the literature develops the advocacy argument. This chapter discusses how to survey the literature to build the discovery argument. To begin, what does a literature survey do?

The literature survey locates, examines, and assesses the field's prior knowledge about the subject of study. Surveying begins with assembling the information from a literature search. It then examines the assembled information to create patterns of evidence—the findings. The survey process concludes by building the findings into the discovery argument, which describes what is known about the topic under study. Surveying requires three tasks (Figure 4.1):

- Task 1. Assemble the collected data.
- Task 2. Organize the information.
- Task 3. Analyze the patterns of the data.

Figure 4.1   Literature Survey Process

Survey Stages	Tasks
Stage 1. Assemble the collected data.	Catalog and document major works of recognized importance—journals, texts, etc. Build lists of authors. Catalog citations. Review the quality and strength of the information. Create survey tally matrix. Document core ideas.
Stage 2. Organize the information.	Arrange and categorize major works into categories—by author, key descriptor and theme, chronology, theory, etc. Organize core maps and outlines according to theme patterns. Expand tentative author maps, theory maps, bibliographic entry card abstracts, and notes to build prevailing theories, principles, etc. Build simple claims.
Stage 3. Analyze the patterns of the data.	Examine core maps and tally matrices to formulate an argument scheme and reasoning pattern to determine "what is known" about the research topic. Create a storyline. Mind map and outline discovery argument. Build complex arguments and major claims. Compose an exploratory document on the current state of knowledge about the research subject. "Tell the story."

TASK 1. ASSEMBLE THE COLLECTED DATA

The literature survey begins with assembling the information gathered from the literature search—Task 1. Careful cataloging provides the opportunity for patterns to appear, and organization can then follow. Use a map or matrix scheme to document your progress through the three tasks. While doing so, construct a central control document to assemble, organize, and analyze the data. You can design this document in varying styles and formats depending on individual need. Figure 4.2 is an example.

Figure 4.2, the literature survey tally matrix, lays out the steps and tasks required to complete the literature survey. The matrix will be a reference for the remainder of this chapter.

Activity 1: Cataloging the Data

At the end of the literature search, you built subject maps, core maps, and bibliographic entry cards. Using those data, assemble this information in a document for review and organization.

Begin the assembly task by cataloging the data compiled from the bibliographic entry cards or data management software onto the matrix. Using Figure 4.2 as a guide, record relevant data for each entry in Columns 1, 2, and 3. Now conduct a quality review of the data gathered. Do the data meet quality standards? As needed, review Chapter 2 for the specific standards used to assess data quality and relevance. Record your assessment of quality in Column 4.

Resist the tendency to transcribe the entirety of the material to the tally matrix. This would be too cumbersome. Here are three alternatives to total transcription of the data:

1. Use coding for cross-referencing the source documents and the central documents. The simplest method is to assign an alphabetic code by author or text. You can use abbreviations or keywords to record the core ideas in the selection review and abstract sections. The important notion here is that the key ideas be decipherable on the tally matrix and that tallying does not become an impossible task. When using a coding scheme, ensure that all information can easily refer back to the original source.

2. Use the reporting function found in software programs such as Citation, EndNote, or RefWorks. Each of these programs can query, search, and report while generating tally documents. When using these digital programs, you can edit and tailor the electronic reports to include the parts of the tally matrix not addressed by the software. Once all the references are recorded in the first four columns of the tally matrix, you can begin analyzing the data, building evidence, and developing claims.

Figure 4.2   Literature Survey Tally Matrices

	Task 1. Assemble the collected data.				Task 2. Organize the information.				Task 3. Analyze the patterns of data.		
	Key concept or descriptor (1)	Citation or reference (2)	Main ideas (3)	Data quality (4)	Evidence categories (5)	Warrant scheme and simple arguments (6)	Simple claim statement (7)	Claim acceptability (8)	Simple claim statement (premises) (9)	Warrant scheme and complex argument (10)	Complex claim statement (11)
	Taken from maps and bibliographic entry card	Taken from maps and bibliographic entry card	Taken from maps and bibliographic entry card	Do data meet quality standards? (yes or no)	Data entry placement into a body of evidence	Warrant scheme used for this evidence group	Data entry is evidence for this claim	Does claim meet acceptability standards? (yes or no)	Simple claim placement as an evidence statement for the major claim	Warrant scheme used to justify the complex argument	The major claims for the discovery argument. The premises of the advocacy argument
Author Text Periodical (A)											
Author Text Periodical (B)											
Author Text Periodical (C)											
Author Text Periodical (n)											

3. Use butcher paper or large sticky notes to assemble the data using storyboard techniques to develop your findings. For our purposes, a storyboard is a graphic organizer, a pictorial outline that displays, sequences, and classifies data into logical patterns for the purpose of being able to visualize and build the elements of evidence necessary for making claims about what is known about the topic of study. When using this alternative, you can directly transcribe the data in longhand or cut and paste data to the storyboard. Web-based programs such as Spaaze or Scrivener provide good digital options for storyboarding.

You can also use a combination of these options to suit your individual skills and preferences.

TASK 2. ORGANIZE THE INFORMATION

Activity 1. Arranging Information to Build Evidence

In Task 1 of the literature survey, you assembled the data collected by the literature search. Task 2 now patterns the data to form a body of evidence to create simple claims. To start, examine the entries made on the tally matrix (Columns 1–3) to determine how the data fit together. Remember, *evidence* is data with a purpose. How are the data combining to tell the story? Examine the data contained on the tally matrix by key descriptor, core idea, or author to develop a picture of the data entries as evidence (Figure 4.3).

Use your core idea maps, author maps, and storyboards to assist in building the data entry picture. Perhaps grouping the entries is best done by time period. If so, organize the matrix data chronologically. Alternatively, the evidence might best be organized by theme. If so, combine bodies of evidence thematically for purposes of comparison or modeling. Finally, you might want to group data into an evidence pattern by various authors to discover trends or characteristics of a topic.

There are many ways to organize data into evidence. The decision about how to organize data will depend on the nature of the subject of study. Again, you need not limit yourself to the use of one evidence pattern. Trying different groupings allows you to examine how best to produce the body of evidence. Perhaps a combination of data groupings is the most suitable method for patterning the data.

As evidence patterns form, document them, and stay up-to-date with your memoranda. Develop a coding scheme to catalog the evidence. The coding scheme should employ keywords or alphanumeric symbols as codes for organizing the evidence. Use a code sheet to list each of the code entries with a short statement describing its identified evidence group.

Figure 4.3 Literature Survey Tally Matrix: Task 1

	Task 1. Assemble the collected data.			
	Key concept or descriptor (1)	Citation or reference (2)	Main ideas (3)	Data quality (4)
	Taken from maps and bibliographic entry card	*Taken from maps and bibliographic entry card*	*Taken from maps and bibliographic entry card*	*Do data meet quality standards? (yes or no)*
Author **Text** **Periodical (A)**				
Author **Text** **Periodical (B)**				
Author **Text** **Periodical (C)**				
Author **Text** **Periodical (n)**				

Enter the codes for evidence categories in Column 5 on the tally matrix. The code sheet is an indispensable reference for further work.

Refer back to Figure 3.10 for an example of how data can be mapped for coding. The key descriptor, "History of the Theory of Intelligence," is in five major parts. A chronological scheme organizes the data. Each of the five major parts is further divided into subsections. For purposes of demonstration, here are codes for the first major part, entitled "Intelligence as an Abstraction (Pre-1910)." Use "pre-1910" as a code for the major part. Use "EGT" as a code to catalog data belonging to the "Early Greek Thought" subcategory and "IPI" as code to catalog data belonging to "Islamic Persian Influences." You can develop the initialing for the contents of the entire core map. The code sheet should note the titles of the major parts and subcategories and the matching abbreviations, which are now available for future reference. Continue this process until you have completed coding and organizing all the data.

At this point of the survey, you have organized data into patterns of evidence, which you now need to warrant. Now you employ reasoning. Conduct a careful analysis to form evidence using an acceptable reasoning pattern. This creates a warranting scheme that justifies the simple claim. The key to success at this critical stage is the ability to see that reasoning pattern.

Reasoning Patterns

Whether unraveling the plot of a good detective novel or assembling a jigsaw puzzle, the reasoning is the same as that used to create the literature review. There are basic patterns in any of these scenarios, and they can be used to organize research evidence and claims to form the argument of discovery. Before you proceed to the next task, here are the patterns you need to understand. Alec Fisher, in *The Logic of Real Arguments* (2003) and *Critical Thinking: An Introduction* (2004), classifies the basic reasoning patterns into four types: (1) one-on-one reasoning, (2) side-by-side reasoning, (3) chain reasoning, and (4) joint reasoning.

These patterns of reasoning move from the simple to the complex. Each pattern serves as a potential organizer for the logical patterning of the connections between data groupings. These patterns are the warranting schemes for connecting evidence to claims.

One-on-One Reasoning

The most elementary reasoning pattern is a simple connection between reasoning and a conclusion. Its diagram is:

$$R \therefore C$$

In this simple pattern, one reason (R) is enough to justify the conclusion (C) (as shown in Figure 4.4). This one-on-one reasoning can be proven as true or false. An example of this type of reasoning would be, "The noon bell has rung. Therefore, it must be lunchtime."

Here you have one datum that convincingly leads to the claim. The map (Figure 4.4) depicts the one-on-one logic—one datum to justify the claim.

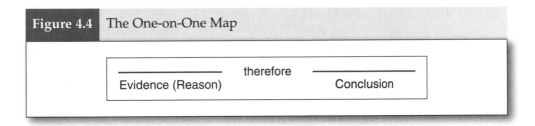

Figure 4.4	The One-on-One Map

Evidence (Reason)   therefore   Conclusion

Side-by-Side Reasoning

A side-by-side reasoning pattern cites several data entries, all of which offer the same reason to justify the conclusion. Here is a diagram of the side-by-side pattern:

$$R_1, R_2, R_3, R_4 \ldots R_n \therefore C.$$

This is the pattern used as an example of warranting reasoning used in Chapter 2, and it is the scheme social science researchers often use in arguing claims for a literature review. This pattern typically uses several authors or theorists in support of the claim; expert opinions, research studies, statistics, expert testimony, and other data all point to the same conclusion. An evidentiary pattern is built as one would build a stone wall. The result, as shown in Figure 4.5, is a collection of overwhelming evidence warranting the conclusion. Side-by-side reasoning is diagrammed using a convergent map.

Convergent maps are cumulative in their logic, which is an apt pattern to use when several data entries independently confirm the conclusion. This is a justified claim because of the sheer number of confirming entries. For example: "The evening news forecasts rain; the barometer says it will rain; the Internet forecast predicts rain; therefore, it will probably rain."

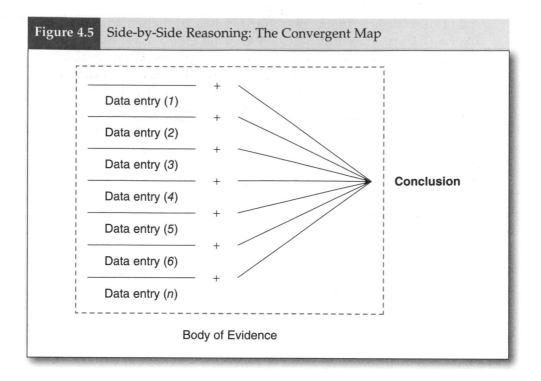

Figure 4.5   Side-by-Side Reasoning: The Convergent Map

Chain Reasoning

Chain reasoning is another pattern researchers widely use in building an argument. Serial in nature, it begins by citing one or more reasons that justify a conclusion. It uses a one-on-one reasoning pattern as its foundation. The conclusion of the first pattern then becomes the evidence for the second conclusion. This line of logic continues until the final conclusion has been warranted. Here is the diagram for a chain-reasoning pattern:

$$(R_1 \therefore C_1) + (C_1 \therefore C_2) + (C_2 \therefore C_3) + \ldots (C_{n-1}) \therefore C_n.$$

Notice that this pattern forms as if you were making a daisy chain (Figure 4.6). Each link of the chain becomes the premise for arguing the next conclusion. The thought pattern is, "If this, then that; because of *a*, then *b*; because of *b*, then *c*." Each conclusion thus becomes the reason that builds the next conclusion, continuing the reasoning pattern.

You can use chain reasoning to link or develop connections among reasons to form an overall conclusion. In chain reasoning, the claim of one set of data will have a bearing on the claim of another set of data. These linkages can be a qualification of one claim on another, a causal connection between claims, an association between claims, or an evolutionary connection of one claim to the next. This mapping scheme is useful in tracking chronological data entries and theory development. For example: "Car engines burn less gas when they work at lower speeds, so lower speeds mean less gas consumption; less gas consumption means fewer toxic fuel emissions; fewer toxic fuel emissions mean less air pollution; therefore, reducing the speed limit means less air pollution."

Figure 4.6 Chain Reasoning

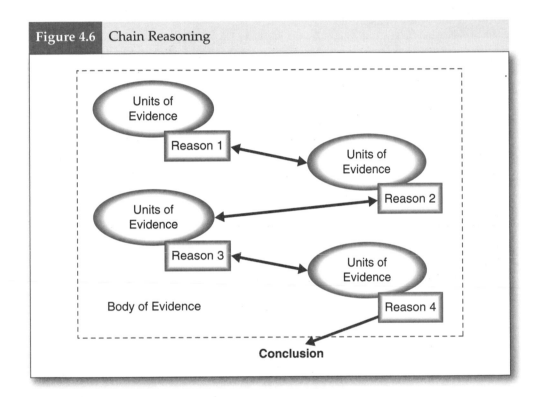

Joint Reasoning

In this case, the reasons stipulated cannot stand on their own but, when taken together, provide the necessary reasoning to warrant the conclusion. A diagram of a joint reasoning pattern is as follows:

$$(R_1 + R_2) \therefore C.$$

Neither R_1 nor R_2 alone provides enough justification to form the conclusion. However, R_1 and R_2 together allow a logically drawn conclusion. This thought pattern is demonstrated in the following manner: "If x exists, and y exists, then z." If one of the partial reasons (x or y) is not present, then there is no justified conclusion. Review the following example: "When the temperature falls below freezing and enough moisture is present, it will probably snow."

Use joint reasoning when you find that data entries build a theory or a position (Figure 4.7). The logic for this map is additive in nature. Notice that the individual datum each entry represents does not justify the conclusion on its own merit. Only when the entries combine can the conclusion be made. The data are parts that together make up a theory or position.

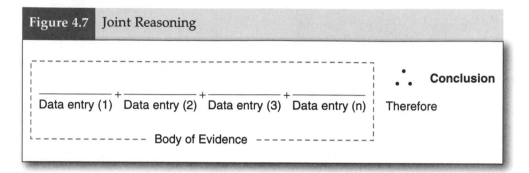

Figure 4.7   Joint Reasoning

Activity 2. Organizing the Information and Building Claims

Applying the previously discussed reasoning patterns as warranting schemes to your evidence groups will produce justified claims. To create a simple claim, transcribe your work on the tally matrix section, as shown in Figure 4.8.

1. Begin by reviewing each data grouping by evidence category. Examine how the data fit together. Then, apply the correct reasoning pattern to each evidence group.

2. Record the reasoning pattern (warranting scheme) for each data group in Column 6 of your tally matrix.

3. Find the conclusion deduced from each of the organized patterns of evidence. Write it as a declarative sentence. This is your claim.

4. In Column 7, write the claim or assertion created by the evidence.

5. After completing your claim statements, evaluate the acceptability of each claim. Is it on point, powerful, supportable, and clearly stated? (Refer to the section on acceptability of claims and Figure 2.3 in Chapter 2.)

6. Record your claim evaluation in Column 8.

The preliminary work of building simple arguments is complete. You have organized and gathered your information into strong bodies of evidence that produced acceptable claims. Now find the connections that exist among the simple claims in order to build the complex argument for what is known about the research subject.

Figure 4.8 Literature Survey Tally Matrix: Task 2

	Task 2. Organize the Information.			
	Evidence categories (5)	Warrant scheme and simple arguments (6)	Simple claim statement (7)	Claim acceptability (8)
	Data entry placement into a body of evidence	*Warrant scheme used for this evidence group*	*Data entry is evidence for this claim*	*Does claim meet acceptability standards? (yes or no)*
Author Text Periodical (A)				
Author Text Periodical (B)				
Author Text Periodical (C)				
Author Text Periodical (n)				

EXERCISE 4.1

Practice in Organizing Data and Building Claims

Use your research to practice organizing data and building claims. Select a key descriptor from your work. Create a shortened version of Figure 4.2 (the literature survey tally matrix) and complete Columns 1 through 4 using the data you have collected. For Columns 5 through 8, follow the tasks listed in Task 2.

TASK 3. ANALYZE THE PATTERNS OF THE DATA

To explain what is known about the subject, build the discovery argument. Make this argument by arranging the simple claims you developed in Column 7 of the tally matrix from Task 2 into a complex argument. This task demands analysis, which is the purpose of Task 3 of the literature survey.

Analysis begins by reviewing the simple claims created in Task 2 to discover their logical pattern. This pattern will present the claims in a reasoned order—a warrant scheme. The simple claims will form a complex argument; the major claims produced become premises for the advocacy argument.

Critically analyze the evidence and claims by asking the following questions: "What do these data say?" "What's the story?" "How do the facts fit together?" Like the chief detective in a good mystery novel, you must unravel the plot by examining the evidence to decide what happened and who did it. Analysis of the evidence by combining the claims in some significant way enables you to compose the story—to make the argument. Using the argument schemes as guides, you can either outline or map the argument. The outline enables you to compose an exploratory draft as the first effort to tell the story of what is known about the subject of the research. If you are new to exploratory writing, or if you need to review it, read the explanation and exercise in Chapter 6, found under the exploratory writing section in Activity 2.

Complex Reasoning

Researchers often use complex reasoning to organize claims into complex arguments. This warranting scheme employs two or more of the four basic reasoning patterns—one-on-one reasoning, side-by-side reasoning, chain reasoning, and joint reasoning—to build the central argument. A complex pattern combines the basic patterns as building blocks to organize the premises that form the discovery argument. The basics for the complex argument are in Chapter 2, with Concept 7 on multiple claims arguments.

Review Figure 2.5 as a reminder. Two regularly used complex warranting schemes that build arguments of discovery are divergent reasoning and comparative reasoning.

Divergent Reasoning

This pattern depicts an academic debate. Divergent reasoning is an off-shoot of the basic side-by-side reasoning pattern:

$$R_1, R_2, R_3, R_4 \ldots R_n \therefore C_A \text{ versus } R_1, R_2, R_3, R_4 \ldots R_n \therefore C_B.$$

Cite several expert opinions, research studies, statistics, expert testimony, and other data in a way that builds an evidentiary pattern for one side of the question. Next, cite another set of data to show the opposing view.

Divergent Mapping

The pattern in Figure 4.9 maps opposing viewpoints. Use this pattern to depict authors' positions, research findings, or theories found in the evidentiary data that are in direct contradiction. By mapping the opposing data, you can graph the vantage point and the focus of each position to discover the strong and weak points for each side of the debate.

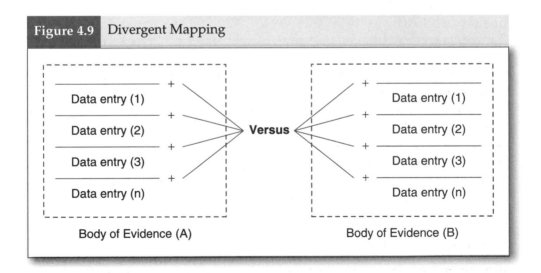

Figure 4.9 Divergent Mapping

Comparative Reasoning

The comparative reasoning scheme shows connections between groups of data. Here you are examining likenesses and differences in each group by comparing and contrasting the evidence and claims associated with each position. This complex reasoning pattern looks like the following formula:

$$R_1, R_2, R_3, R_4 \ldots R_n \therefore C_A \wedge R_1, R_2, R_3, R_4 \ldots R_n \therefore C_B.$$

As with side-by-side reasoning, cite expert opinions, research studies, statistics, expert testimony, and other data to build an evidentiary pattern for the first claim group (A). The set of data from the next claim group (B) is also presented. Look at the differences and likenesses between the data presented, and compare and contrast the two side-by-side arguments. You can graphically represent this reasoning by using a Venn diagram (Figure 4.10).

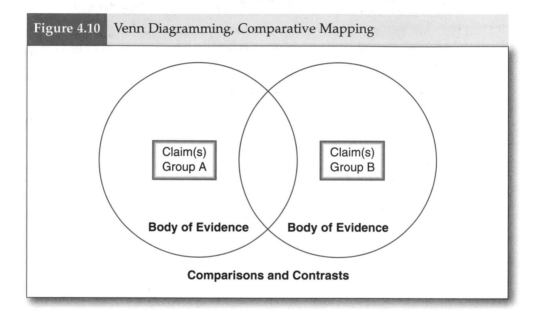

| Figure 4.10 | Venn Diagramming, Comparative Mapping |

Venn diagrams map the connections between two or more data groups. They are commonly used when charting the relationships between theoretical data, opposing positions, two populations, or alternative methods. Each circle in the Venn diagram represents one body of evidence. Once you have described each claim, you can easily show the commonalities of the combined claims by noting those parts of each claim that fall inside the circles' intersection. To see the differences, note those parts that fall outside the intersection.

The Discovery Argument: Putting It All Together

You should now understand the reasoning used to warrant and map both simple and complex arguments. How do we construct and depict the discovery argument? The complex argument, as defined in Chapter 2, provides the framework for understanding how the discovery argument is made. Figure 4.11 below shows how the complex argument is built. The literature is surveyed in Tasks 1 and 2. Data are assembled in Task 1 and categorized into main ideas or elements in Task 2. These become the evidence for a simple claim(s). In Task 3, the patterns of the data are organized

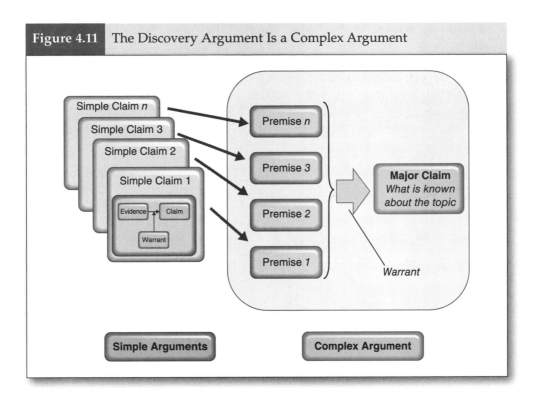

Figure 4.11 The Discovery Argument Is a Complex Argument

and analyzed to become the premises for the major claim(s) of the complex argument. The warranting schemes provided in this chapter are the logics used to legitimately conclude the major claim(s). In the case of a literature review, the major claim(s) answers the question, "What is known about the subject of study?"

Building the Discovery Argument: An Example

The following is an example of the use of complex reasoning to form a discovery argument about a topic of study. Suppose the subject of study is, "The Definition of Human Intelligence in the 20th Century: A Cognitive Perspective." The literature survey documents the seminal works on the subject. After completing the appraisal activities in surveying the literature, three positions emerge:

1. Human intelligence consists of a single structure, as opposed to the position that human intelligence consists of multiple structures of several domains or dimensions.

2. Human intelligence can be accurately measured, as opposed to the position that human intelligence cannot be accurately measured.

3. Human intelligence is inherited and static, as opposed to the position that human intelligence is changeable and developmental.

Perhaps the researcher mapped the first theme—single versus multiple intelligences—as shown in Figure 4.12.

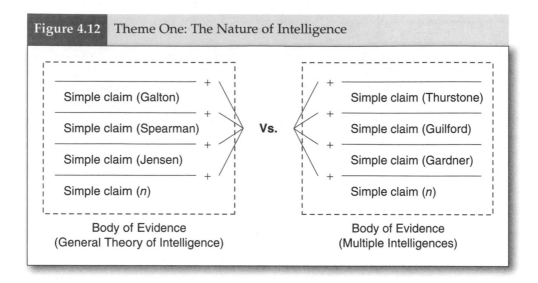

Figure 4.12 Theme One: The Nature of Intelligence

This researcher selected divergent mapping as the scheme to organize the data. As shown in the figure, multiple simple arguments make up the body of evidence for both theories of intelligence. To build the argument, begin by developing each of the simple arguments of the scheme. Notice that in this case each simple argument depends on the theory of a specific author.

To continue the example, map and pattern a simple argument for each competing theory: Spearman's theory for the general theory of intelligence and Gardner's theory for multiple intelligences. A simple map can chart Spearman's theory of intelligence, and a one-on-one reasoning pattern explains his theory:

$$R \therefore C.$$

Positive Manifold = Intelligence Level.

Spearman declared that one single general cause governs the intelligence of an individual. He called that general cause a *positive manifold* (which he defines in his work).

Chain reasoning diagrams this theory as follows:

$$(R_1 \therefore C_1) + (C_1 \therefore C_2).$$

In narrative form, you can express this theory as follows: If certain parts of the brain can map with certain cognitive functioning, then that cognitive role can be isolated as one of the multiple intelligences. Certain parts of the brain distinctively map with certain cognitive functioning; therefore, there are multiple intelligences.

Gardner has identified eight specific intelligences that identify with unique human cognitive functions of intelligence. He has determined each of these intelligences based on the chain reasoning used in Figure 4.12. Assume that the theory offered by each of the authors was reasoned as a simple argument. You must now develop a reasoning pattern for the complex argument.

You continue using divergent mapping as the overall scheme for the argument. Side-by-side reasoning builds the body of evidence for both the general theory of intelligence and the theory of multiple intelligences. It is diagrammed as follows:

$$R_1, R_2, R_3, R_4 \ldots R_n \therefore C_A \text{ versus } R_1, R_2, R_3, R_4 \ldots R_n \therefore C_B.$$

Using the cumulative scheme of side-by-side reasoning, you compile each of the simple arguments as separate reasons for justifying the conclusion. Combining the arguments by Spearman, Galton, Jensen, and others produces the body of evidence that proposed the claim for the general theory of intelligence. Compiling the work of Guilford, Thurston, Gardner, and others in the same fashion produces the evidence for the theory of multiple intelligences.

Reasoning patterns are invaluable aids in developing arguments for a literature survey. First, simple reasoning patterns are applied to form simple arguments and claims. These claims now become premises and are organized as evidence for the complex argument. Complex reasoning patterns are used again to determine the warranting scheme that justifies the major claim of the complex argument. To build the complex reasoning for the discovery argument, use Task 3 of the tally matrix (Figure 4.13).

Activity 1. Mapping the Discovery Argument

To begin the analysis, review the claims posted in Column 8. Reorganize these claims using complex reasoning patterns. Regroup the corresponding arguments for each claim by these patterns. Now record the reordered claims, stating them as premises in Column 9. Analyze the premises made in Column 9. Determine the reasoning pattern that will serve as the warranting scheme for the complex claim (thesis) of the discovery argument. State the warrant scheme in Column 10. Write the thesis statement for the discovery argument in Column 11.

Activity 2. Analyzing the Argument

Once you have completed the literature survey and mapped and outlined the argument for what is known, evaluate the argument's soundness using Exercise 4.2.

Figure 4.13 Literature Survey Tally Matrix: Task 3

	Task 3. Analyze the patterns of the data.		
	Simple claim statement (premises) (9)	**Warrant scheme and complex argument (10)**	**Complex claim statement (11)**
	Simple claim placement as an evidence statement for the major claim	*Warrant scheme used to justify the complex argument*	*The major claims for the discovery argument. The premises of the advocacy argument*
Author **Text** **Periodical (A)**			
Author **Text** **Periodical (B)**			
Author **Text** **Periodical (C)**			
Author **Text** **Periodical (n)**			

EXERCISE 4.2

Evaluating an Argument

Evaluating the Simple Argument

1. Are your simple claims soundly reasoned? That is, do the simple arguments posed create a simple claim supported by evidence and a valid warrant? Refer back to Chapter 2, Concept 2.

2. Is each claim properly supported by evidence? How do you know? Refer to Chapter 2, Concept 5.

3. Is each of the simple arguments correctly warranted by sound reasoning patterns that justify each claim made? Refer to Chapter 2, Concept 6.

4. Are there any disconnected claims or evidentiary statements? Do they need warranting or discarding?

Evaluating the Complex Argument

1. What is the complex argument for your thesis?

2. What premises make up the complex argument?

3. How are the premises warranted to conclude the thesis?

4. What is the logic scheme of your argument? What reasoning pattern is used (joint, side by side, chain)? Is the complex argument logical? What is its warrant?

5. Is anything out of place? Are there simple claims that are irrelevant to the argument? Note them. Avoid both "red herring" statements that provide off-topic information and "rabbit-run commentary" that strays from the subject of the topic by following tangential information.

Tips

1. Make sure that you have completed a comprehensive search before beginning your literature survey.

2. Use some form of tally matrix to storyboard your arguments. The tally matrix is both an organizational and a critical-thinking tool. Whatever form you use, be sure to take advantage of both features.

3. Learn the reasoning patterns so they will be available as needed. These patterns are critical to assembling good arguments.

SUMMARY

The literature survey is the discovery of what is known about the subject of research. To conduct a literature survey, first develop a tally matrix to examine the data, and then conduct a final check on the truth of the evidence collected. Next, organize and group the data entries from the tally matrix into evidence to develop the claims. Build the groups chronologically, thematically, or in combination. Once you build the groups, compose the reasoning patterns and maps to create simple arguments. Build and organize simple claims into the premises of the major argument. You are now able to build the discovery argument.

You have now completed the literature survey. The argument of discovery for what is known about the subject of research is in place. The first argument, or the front end, of the research case is done. However, what are the implications of what is known about the research subject? Does what is known about the research subject answer your original inquiry? Are there gaps, omissions, debates, and questions about the topic that need further study? Given what is known about the subject of the research, what can you conclude? These are all questions that ask you to critique the present knowledge on the topic. We address the second argument that is needed to complete the research case in the next chapter.

CHECKLIST

Task	Completed
Assemble the Data	
1. Create a survey tally matrix.	☐
2. Catalog and document major works of recognized importance.	☐
3. Build authors lists.	☐
4. Catalog citations.	☐
5. Organize data into categories by theme.	☐
6. Bracket main ideas by theme category.	☐
7. Review the quality and strength of the data.	☐
Organize the Data	
1. Organize core maps and outlines according to theme patterns.	☐
2. Create an historical log of scan process.	☐

3. Arrange all maps, main idea cards, key words, and notes to build evidence categories. ☐

4. Apply a warrant scheme to each theme group. ☐

Analyze the Claims

1. Examine the maps and the tally matrix to formulate a complex argument scheme. ☐

2. Outline the discovery argument. ☐

3. Apply a warrant scheme to the discovery argument. ☐

4. Build complex arguments and major claims. These are the major claim(s) that become the premise(s) for the argument of advocacy. ☐

REFLECTIVE OVERSIGHT

1. Have I created a usable survey tally matrix for my data? If not, how do I rework this?

2. Do I continue to be successful in filling in the tally matrix?

3. Have I been able to form my claims into complex arguments that have built the discovery argument?

Step 5. Critique the Literature

5

Step Five:
Critique the Literature

Interpreting the Research

Botte buona fa buon vino.
A good cask makes good wine.

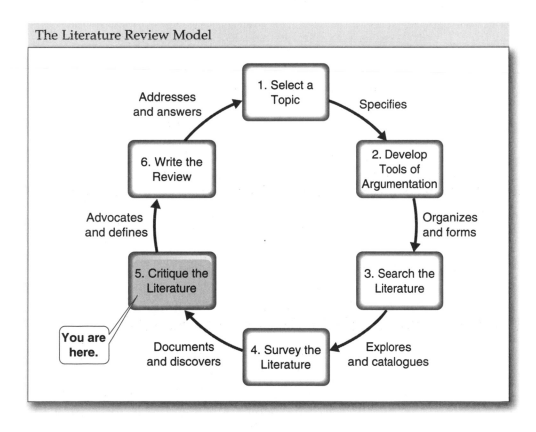

The Literature Review Model

KEY VOCABULARY

- **Backing**—That which justifies the warrant.

- **Descriptive Reasoning**—A process that examines data in order to identify or explain a phenomenon. It follows an if/then pattern. The *then* part is true when the *if* part has been proven.

- **Fallacy**—An argument that leads to an erroneous or misleading conclusion.

- **Implicative Reasoning**—Reasoning that logically interprets evidence, producing propositions that signal a specific conclusion. If A is true, then we can assert that B is also true.

- **Literature Critique**—Interprets the current understanding of the research topic and logically determines how this knowledge answers the research question.

- **Thesis**—A conclusion based on a case developed using existing knowledge, sound evidence, and reasoned argument.

The discovery argument is now developed and has solid findings. Isn't it time to write the review? After all, don't we have our conclusions?

CHAPTER OVERVIEW

There is a difference between findings and conclusions. Findings are the facts about the subject in question. Conclusions are the legitimate positions or the actions to be taken that logically follow from an examination of the findings. When reviewing the critical-thinking process (see the Introduction), we see findings must be critically analyzed to create a logical argument that leads to a warranted conclusion. Well-argued findings only provide the facts of the case. We now must take the next step and answer the question, "Now that we have the facts about the case, so what?" In other words, given the findings, what legitimate conclusions can be drawn to address the topic query? Step 5, the critique of the literature, conducts this analysis, producing the advocacy argument and its resulting thesis statement.

   This chapter defines the process of critiquing the literature. It addresses the descriptive and implicative reasoning needed to draw logical conclusions. Nine logic patterns are presented for use in constructing advocacy arguments. The conditional rules, which are the criteria for testing the legitimacy of these logics, are also provided. The chapter closes with a discussion of the pitfalls and fallacies that create fallacious arguments.

WHAT IS A LITERATURE CRITIQUE?

Critiquing is the art of interpreting the meaning of a piece of literary, scientific, or technical work. A critique develops a well-founded argument stemming from a detailed analysis and assessment of the work. A **literature critique** interprets the current understanding of the research topic and logically determines how this knowledge answers the research question. The critique answers the question, "Given what I know now, what is the legitimate response to the question posed by the study topic?" The analysis made in response to this question creates the advocacy argument and the resulting thesis of the literature review. The literature review is completed when a thesis position can be legitimately drawn based on an analysis of current knowledge about the topic.

Most class assignments and master's studies require a simple literature review. The critique of the literature creates a thesis statement that takes a position on what is currently known about the subject of study. Projects such as doctoral dissertations and some master's theses use the complex literature review, however, and demand thesis statements that extend topic knowledge beyond what is known by uncovering a new research question and a new research problem to study. The researcher must ask more questions. What new research would logically extend present knowledge? What are the gaps, contradictions, omissions, and debates about the research subject that were uncovered by the discovery argument? The literature critique must go further than just advocating what is now known about the subject. Its argument of advocacy must define what is known and also logically identify and define a new unanswered question—a significant question requiring new primary research.

Whether dealing with a thesis that interprets what is known about the study topic or a thesis that identifies a new problem for research, the researcher must present a sound argument of advocacy that justifies the thesis claim.

CONCEPT 1. MAKING THE CASE FOR THE LITERATURE REVIEW

As learned earlier, the literature review case is made by linking the advocacy argument with the discovery argument. The chain-reasoning logic scheme is used to create this link.

Chain reasoning is the logical pattern for diagramming the if/then argument used to build the case for a literature review. Do you remember how chain reasoning is constructed? If you need a refresher, see Chapter 4. Figure 5.1 diagrams how the literature review case is made using chain reasoning. Notice that the first argument is constructed citing certain facts as evidence ($R_1 \ldots R_n$), logically leading to the conclusions (C_1).

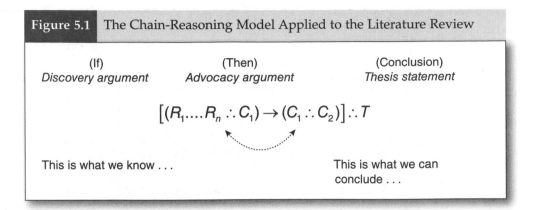

Figure 5.1   The Chain-Reasoning Model Applied to the Literature Review

(If)	(Then)	(Conclusion)
Discovery argument	*Advocacy argument*	*Thesis statement*

$$[(R_1....R_n \therefore C_1) \rightarrow (C_1 \therefore C_2)] \therefore T$$

This is what we know . . .   This is what we can
                                                                    conclude . . .

The conclusions drawn from the first argument become the evidence (C_1) for the second argument. When properly warranted, this evidence leads to the next conclusion (C_2). (C_2) conclusions are rewritten to directly address the question posed, thereby creating the thesis (T).

Figure 5.2 diagrams how chain reasoning builds the case for the literature review. During the literature survey, the argument of discovery is built. The argument of advocacy is made by doing the literature critique. Notice that the complex claims justified in the argument of discovery are the foundational evidence for the advocacy argument of the literature critique. The argument of advocacy produces the *then* of an if/then argument. If the major claims found by the argument of discovery are true, then you must conclude the following answer (**thesis**) to the research question.

Since all research is developed on a continuum that moves from identification to explanation to prediction to control, research questions can be framed based on each of these four categories. Questions seeking the identification of, or an explanation about, the subject phenomena require a descriptive response and use a factual line of reasoning. Questions seeking to predict or control phenomena seek an inferential response and employ an implicative line of reasoning.

Because the line of questioning determines the argument of advocacy posed by the research question, the reasoning pattern must mirror that line to satisfy the question. Two lines of reasoning, descriptive and implicative, can be used to develop the advocacy warrant. The choice of these lines of reasoning is determined by the type of response required by the research question asked.

CONCEPT 2. DESCRIPTIVE ARGUMENT PATTERNS: FACTUAL REASONING

Much of the research conducted in social science seeks to describe the nature of the case rather than predict or control it. Defined, the descriptive

Figure 5.2 The Research Case of the Literature Review

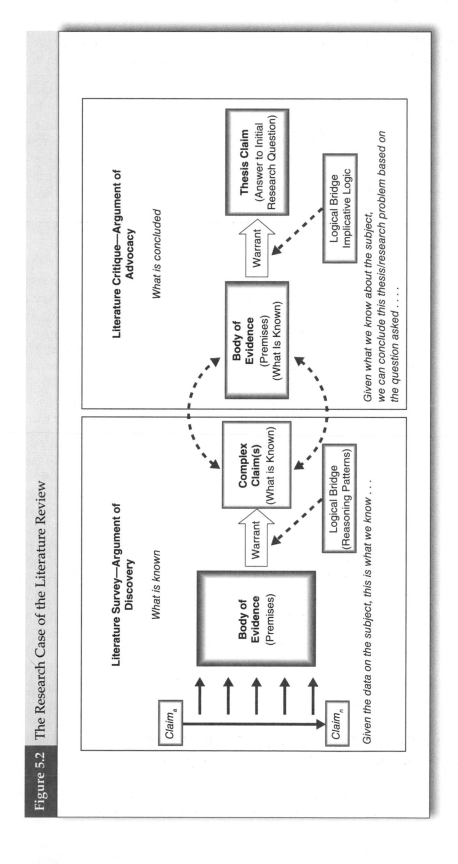

argument follows an if/then pattern, where the *then* part is true whenever the *if* part is true. Comparison or contrast logic schemes are used to form these advocacy arguments.

Convergent and divergent mapping, such as a Venn diagram (see Chapter 4), are employed to organize argument premises. Side-by-side logic patterns serve as the warranting schemes for the descriptive argument. The case made describes how elements identified by the research question, phenomenon (*A*), are alike and/or different. In descriptive arguments, warrant validity relies on the strength authority of the claims that form the premises of the advocacy argument. The authoritative strength of each claim is assessed using the criteria for *claim acceptability*. The strength of the evidence making the claim is judged by its quality and relevance (see Chapter 2).

Descriptive arguments, as discussed in Chapter 4, are really complex arguments relying on the accuracy and adequacy of the evidence to build the claims of fact. The legitimacy of the case made by the advocacy argument depends entirely on the authority of the evidence. Figure 5.3 diagrams the argument of advocacy used to make the descriptive argument.

CONCEPT 3. IMPLICATIVE ARGUMENT PATTERNS: IMPLICATIVE REASONING

Research conducted in the social sciences seeks to develop inferences. These questions are ones of prediction and control. The advocacy argument for inferential questions uses implicative reasoning to reach a conclusion. **Implicative reasoning**, by definition, is a logical interpretation of evidence that produces propositions that signal a specific conclusion, forming a **deductive argument**. If *A* is true, then we can assert that *B* is also true.

Here is a simple example of an if/then case: "If it is raining, then I should take an umbrella when walking to work." Notice there are two arguments in this statement: "if it is raining" and "take an umbrella." Each of the arguments has two independent claims that need separate proofs. The first statement, "if it is raining," needs proof that it is raining. Once it is proven that rain is falling, it is necessary to propose that it would be reasonable to take an umbrella to work. Does the need for an umbrella logically follow? The warrant of the first case (direct observation) comes from using some means of observation to confirm that it is raining. The proven claim that it is raining becomes the premise for the evidence of the second argument: "Given that it is raining, what should I do?" The second argument must logically advocate the implications of the facts to settle on a reasonable action. This argument must show that, because it is raining, you will get wet walking outside. If you prefer to stay dry, you should use an umbrella. This advocacy argument uses an *ends-to-means* reasoning pattern for its justification. "If it is raining and we want to remain dry,

Figure 5.3 The Descriptive Case—Argument of Advocacy

Figure 5.3 The Descriptive Case—Argument of Advocacy

Thesis Claim

The argument of authority used in the discovery argument warrants the advocacy argument and thesis statement.

Simple Claim (1)
Simple Claim (2)
Simple Claim (3)
Simple Claim (n)

Body of evidence
Phenomenon Y

Versus and/or compare

Simple Claim (1)
Simple Claim (2)
Simple Claim (3)
Simple Claim (n)

Body of evidence
Phenomenon X

Premise Statement

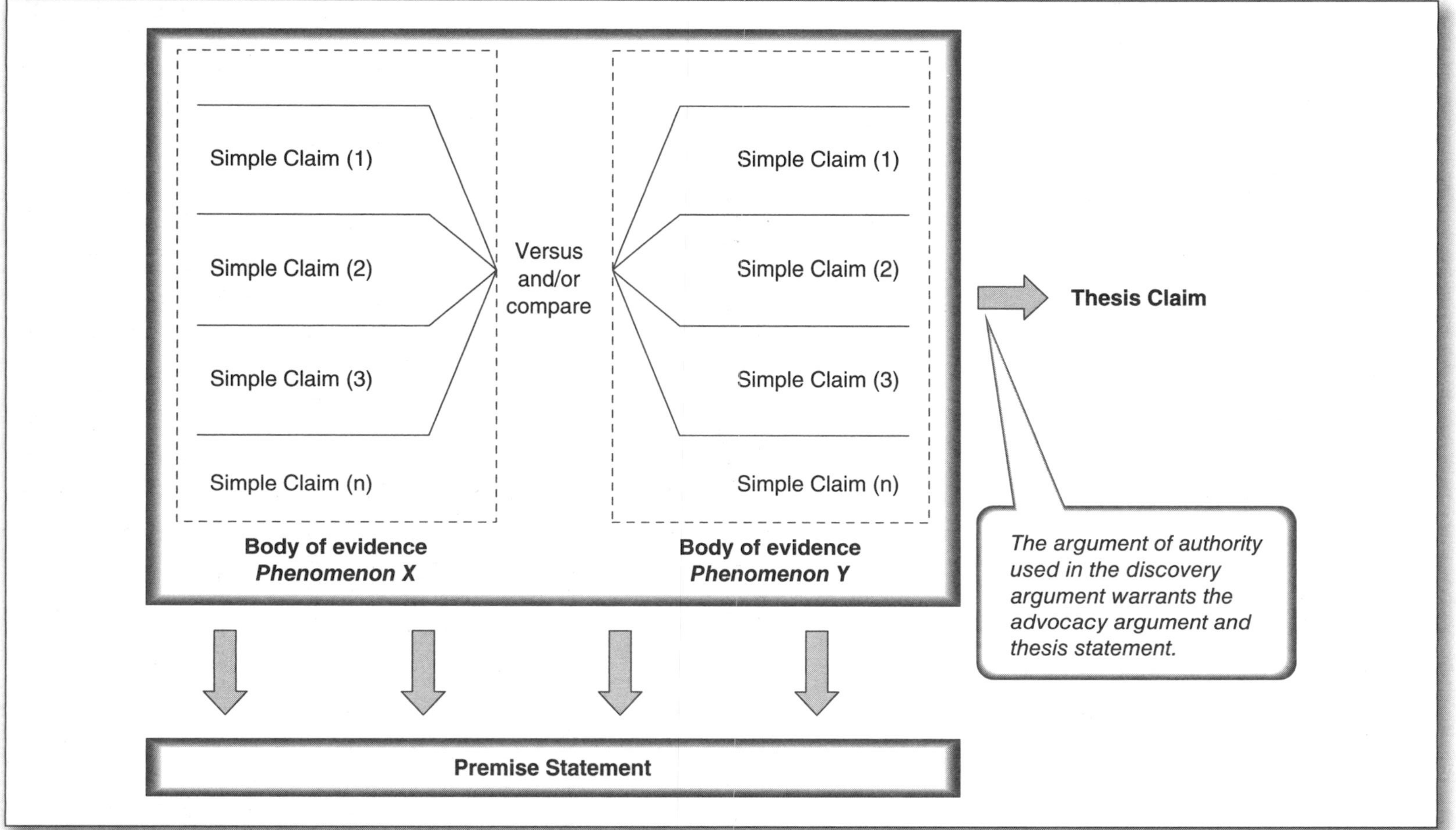

experience suggests that using an umbrella is a suitable means to satisfy the end." The success in supporting the thesis depends upon the implied logic used in the argument.

The backing for the warrant's force is that previous experience has demonstrated that the use of an umbrella can protect a person from the rain. The warrant provided the logical bridge to justify the use of an umbrella as a reasonable conclusion. This example may seem an exercise in too much explanation. However, having broken down each of the steps of this example shows the analytical reasoning used when employing an if/then case.

CONCEPT 4. THE IMPLICATIVE ARGUMENT: NINE BASIC PATTERNS

To build an implicative advocacy argument for the literature critique, ask the following questions: "If the premises stating what is known about the research question are X, then what can I conclude?" "What logical link makes the if/then connection?" "What type of implicative argument will produce a legitimate conclusion?" In his text *Informal Logic: Issues and Techniques* (1997), Wayne Grennan identified nine basic implicative argument patterns based on the work of Ehninger and Brockreide (1960). These nine patterns identify the links between the study question and the claims made by the argument of discovery. A sound rule of logic forms the basis for each pattern. Select the argument pattern that provides the best logical connection between premises and the thesis (conclusion).

The key to selecting the correct pattern is to see the linkage between the type of argument the research question is seeking and the evidence and premises developed by the literature survey. For instance, let's begin with a simplified research question: "What eating habits lead to obesity in children?" The information needed to answer this question is causal to the effect of obesity. The best fit for a logical link is a cause-and-effect connection. Because the question states the effect and asks for the causes, then the argument of discovery must provide premises that state the eating and activity habits that can lead to obesity. The logic of the research question will follow one or more of these argument pattern types. Analyze your question and determine which of the nine argument pattern types fits best. Once you have decided on the correct, logical argument pattern type, then develop the advocacy argument.

Figure 5.4 lists the nine implicative patterns of logic used to form the implicative arguments. Each logic pattern is defined by its rule of logic and is followed by the prerequisite condition that must be satisfied to validate the argument.

Figure 5.4	Nine Patterns of Implicative Argumentation

Argument pattern	Rule of logic	Prerequisite conditions: "The researcher must show that . . ."
Cause and Effect	For every cause there is an effect.	. . . the body of evidence identifies data that are directly causal.
Effect to Cause	Every effect has a cause.	. . . the body of evidence contains the direct effects caused by the case defined in the research question.
Sign	Identifiable symptoms, signals, or signs precede events and actions.	. . . the data identified by the body of evidence are symptomatic of the action or event defined in the research question.
Sample to Population	What is true of the sample is also true of the whole.	. . . the sample identified in the body of evidence is truly representative of the population defined by the research question.
Population to Sample	What is true of the population is also true of a representative part of that whole.	. . . the population identified in the body of evidence is truly representative of the sample defined by the research question.
Parallel Case	Where two cases are similar, what is true of the first case is also true of the second.	. . . the case identified in the body of evidence is similar enough to the case defined by the research question to make them parallel.
Analogy	Because two items are alike, a conclusion drawn from one can be assumed to be a conclusion drawn about the other.	. . . the case identified by the body of evidence contains qualities that provide explanation or clarity to similar qualities contained in the case defined by the research question.
Authority	The more a person knows about an issue, the more factual the claim about that issue.	. . . the testimony presented in the body of evidence uses reliable expert testimony relevant to the case defined by the research question.
Ends–Means	The result is directly attributable to performing a named action.	. . . the action identified in the body of evidence of the literature survey will achieve the ends as identified by the research question.

The list below provides further explanation of the nine implicative logic types with examples of research questions for each.

1. **Cause and Effect.** *Causes lead to effects* is the implied rule of logic that warrants this pattern. To use this argument pattern type, you must show that the body of evidence premises the causes of the effects defined in the research question.

   Examples of research questions using this argument pattern type are

   - *What are the reasons for the high school dropout rate among inner-city minority teens?*
   - *What are the causes of multigenerational welfare dependency?*

   Each question defines an effect and asks for the causes. The premises settled by the discovery argument must provide the causal evidence leading to the thesis argument.

2. **Effect to Cause.** The effect-to-cause argument pattern type uses the reverse logic of cause and effect. The rule states that all effects come from a cause or causes. You can use this argument pattern type when you can show that a body of evidence defines the effects caused by the case defined in the research question.

   Examples of research questions using this argument pattern type are

   - *What are the effects of early intervention programs on teen alcoholism?*
   - *What is the impact of hard-line contract negotiations on employee morale?*

   These research questions state a cause and ask what resulted from that cause. The premises created from the discovery argument must provide the evidence of the effects that lead to the thesis argument.

3. **Sign.** This pattern type works when the research question is seeking legitimate signals, indicators, or symptoms of an event or action. The rule of logic for this argument pattern type is that symptoms, signals, or indicators precede actions or events. The precondition for use of this argument pattern type must show the premises to be the legitimate symptoms, signals, or indicators of the case as defined by the research question.

   Examples of research questions using this argument pattern type are

   - *What are the early warning signs of autism in children?*
   - *What are the qualities of a dysfunctional group?*

   Each of these research questions demands premises that signal the conditions described by the research question. The premises concluded from the discovery argument must provide the symptoms, signals, or indicators as evidence that leads to the thesis argument.

4. **Sample to Population.** When the question of inquiry uses a representative sample of a defined population to determine the qualities of that population, use the sample-to-population argument pattern type. The rule of logic that warrants this argument pattern type states that what is true of the sample is also true of the whole. Thus, the sample identified in the body of evidence actually represents the population defined by the research question. The rule stating that which is true of the sample is also true of the population provides the logical connection that ties the premises to the conclusion.

   Examples of research questions using this argument pattern type are

   - *Based on the SAT results of the past 10 years, are California high school graduates better prepared to attend a university than all other high school graduates from all other states?*
   - *Is a representative sample of students attending universities accredited by the American Bar Association (ABA) better able to pass the bar exam than the general population of students attending universities, based on first-time passage rate for students taking the bar examination?*

   Each of these research questions needs data about a population and about the sample under examination. To apply this argument pattern type, you must be able to show that this sample is actually representative of the population. Claims must use representative samples of the identified population as evidentiary data. When a researcher has met the rule of logic, the premises will show a logical conclusion (thesis) about the population.

5. **Population to Sample.** Population to sample applies when the research question seeks to define or describe a sample or predict its actions using data about the general population. The rule of logic states that what is true of the population is also true of a representative part of that whole. This argument pattern type uses the reverse logic of sample to population. In this argument pattern type, the premises represent the qualities of an entire population and apply to the sample identified by the research question.

   Examples of research questions using this argument pattern type are

   - *What interpersonal communication skills can health professionals use to build cooperative client behavior?*
   - *What leadership strategies can managers employ to foster employee commitment and cooperation?*

   Both of these questions seek premises drawn from evidence about an entire population that is directly attributable to the sample in question. This argument pattern type works when the characteristics of the whole are drawn directly from the representative sample. To use this argument pattern type, it is necessary to show that a sample defined by the research question is actually representative of the population identified by the body of evidence.

6. **Parallel Case.** Many research inquiries ask for comparisons about two identified cases. This argument pattern type works to make the critique argument when the two cases are similar. The parallel case argument pattern type uses the comparison of two like cases for its logic. The rule for the parallel case is where two cases are similar, what is true for the first case is also true for the second.

    Examples of research questions using this argument pattern type are

    - *What teaching strategies employed in selected high-performing schools can be used by other high-performing schools to increase student competence in science?*
    - *What interpersonal skills employed by a sample of effective executive teams can other effective executive teams use to promote positive communications?*

    Each of these research questions uses the likeness of the qualities of the exemplary case as the premise to address the case defined by the research question. To employ this argument pattern type, you must show that a case identified by the body of evidence is similar to the case defined by the research question.

7. **Analogy.** Use an analogy argument pattern type when a research question seeks to clarify or expose the qualities of a particular case by comparing it to an archetype, a prototype, or a stereotype. The analogy argument pattern type also uses the logic of comparison. It compares like parts within a defined case to parts within a prototypical case for purposes of explanation or clarification. This comparison differs from the parallel case in that the parallel case argues the likeness of the two cases. The analogy argues that qualities or parts of the prototype, archetype, or stereotype explain the qualities or parts described by the research question.

    Examples of research questions using this argument pattern type are

    - *How can institutions of higher education compare to the model of a living organism to explain their internal workings?*
    - *How are the steps of building a literature review like assembling a jigsaw puzzle?*

    The previous questions signal the use of an analogy argument pattern type. To employ this argument pattern type, show that a case identified by a body of evidence clarifies and explains something not understood by relating it to that which is familiar.

8. **Authority.** Reference to authority is the most common argument pattern type used in forming a research question. The logic employed depends on reliable expert testimony or observation that directly applies to the case defined in the research question. The rule of logic states that because the expert finds the case to be true, and the expert is a valid source, then it is true.

    Examples of research questions using this argument pattern type are

    - *What is the nature of human intelligence?*
    - *What are the characteristics of effective leadership in complex organizations?*

    These questions can effectively use relevant expert testimony as evidence to justify the conclusion, the thesis of their case. To employ this argument pattern type, show that a case identified by the body of evidence provides the authoritative answer to the question posed by the research question.

9. **Ends-Means.** The research question that asks for a preferable direction, method, or action to take uses the ends-means argument pattern type to form the critique argument. The rule of logic employed states that a result is directly attributable to carrying out a chosen action. Here, the direction or action claimed by the premises will achieve the end sought in the research question.

    Examples of research questions using this argument pattern type are

    - *What interactive skills must a mediator have to conduct a productive third-party intervention?*
    - *What coaching skills are necessary for mentors to work successfully with first-year interns?*

    In each of the previous questions, look for propositions that offer the solution to the issue posed by the research question. To employ this pattern successfully, you must show that the action identified in the body of evidence of the literature survey is designed to achieve the ends as identified by the research question.

Each of these nine argument pattern types provides a logical rule that justifies the premise (evidence) to the claim (conclusion), thus satisfying the basic rules of argumentation. The argument pattern types provide the means to warrant the conclusion for an argument of advocacy, the thesis statement of the literature review.

CONCEPT 5. BACKING

Before leaving the argument pattern types of implicative reasoning, consider one more important notion, **backing,** or that which justifies the warrant. Assume a reasonable implicative pattern developed the argument, but two questions remain: Is the argument pattern type legitimate? Have the prerequisite conditions associated with the argument type been satisfied? Each of the argument pattern types has a rule of logic that makes it operable. Each relies on this rule as a specific condition that you must fulfill to use the argument pattern type correctly. For example, when applying *population to sample,* the rule states that what is true of the population is also true of a representative part of the population. For a researcher to apply this argument pattern type correctly, two prerequisite conditions are necessary to satisfy the underlying rule. These two conditions provide the backing that makes the argument pattern type valid.

1. The part identified must be a valid sample of the population under study.

2. The part identified must be a representative sample of the population under study. *Representative* means the sample represents all qualities of the population.

Without meeting these conditions, the rule of logic that forms the argument pattern type is not valid. Each of the nine argument pattern types has one or more conditional rules that are necessary for applying the argument pattern type correctly. Toulmin (1999), in developing his argumentation theory, calls these conditional rules the backing for the warrant. Backing provides confirmation for the warrant. Reread Figure 5.4 to remind yourself of the necessary prerequisite conditions for the argument pattern types.

Employing the proper argument pattern type creates the logical connection between the research question and the premises formed in the argument of discovery. The argument pattern is the warrant logic for claiming the thesis of the literature review. Building a strong case for the thesis is a major concern for every researcher. While the thesis case will never be perfect, it must be sound. This means that the case, when presented, must withstand rebuttal arguments made against it. Soundness also implies that a community of peers can understand and accept the case premises and thesis.

DOING A CRITIQUE OF THE LITERATURE: BUILDING THE ADVOCACY ARGUMENT

The literature critique consists of three tasks, as shown in Figure 5.5. Task 1 determines the implicative logic sought by the topic of study. Task 2

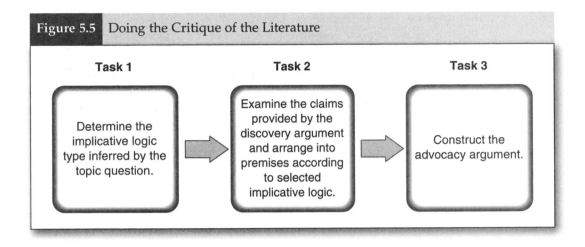

Figure 5.5 Doing the Critique of the Literature

Task 1

Determine the implicative logic type inferred by the topic question.

Task 2

Examine the claims provided by the discovery argument and arrange into premises according to selected implicative logic.

Task 3

Construct the advocacy argument.

requires reframing the claims made by the discovery argument according to the logic type selected in Task 1 to form the premises of the advocacy argument. Once the premises are constructed, Task 3 can be completed by drawing the warranted conclusions according to the selected logic and completing the advocacy argument.

TASK 1. DETERMINING THE IMPLICATIVE LOGIC PATTERN INFERRED BY THE TOPIC OF STUDY

The topic of study can be stated in the form of a question or a declaration. To determine the appropriate implicative logic pattern, look for the keywords in the topic statement or research question that signal the implicative logic needed to form the argument of advocacy. Once these keywords are identified, refer to the nine logic types and select the appropriate one that will make the connection between the claims made in the discovery argument to form the premises of the advocacy argument. Here is an example: "What state and national policies led to the creation of the red state and blue state cultures in the United States at the beginning of the 21st century?"

Look at the verb first to determine what action is defined. In this case, the keyword "led" provides the first clue. The implicative logic pattern is one of cause and effect. Reading the sentence further, we see that we are examining state and national policies as causal factors for this phenomenon. The keywords "red state and blue state cultures" are the effects of these policies. Given these keywords, it is now possible to go to the logic types to find the appropriate implicative logic and prerequisites necessary to warrant the advocacy argument. Reviewing the argument patterns and definitions as shown in Figure 5.4, we are able to identify that the implicative logic inferred by this question is *cause and effect*. The rule of logic for the cause-and-effect case states that for every cause there is an effect. The necessary precondition that must be satisfied by the premises is the body of evidence identifies the national and state policies that have directly caused the effects—red state and blue state cultures.

It is important to note here that many topics of study or research questions are descriptive in nature. These questions tend to look for comparisons and contrasts between and among identified subjects. Here's an example: "Compare the teaching cultures of institutions of higher education in Taiwan with those of the United States."

Parsing the subject of study, notice that the verb *compare* is simply asking for a comparison between two elements, the teaching culture of the institutions of higher education in Taiwan and the teaching culture of institutions of higher education in the United States. Notice we are looking for the similarities and contrasts between these two cultures. *Divergent* and *comparative* complex reasoning patterns are used to form this type of argument.

So, what is the implicative logic pattern used to warrant the example's conclusions? Descriptive cases use the *authority* logic pattern to warrant their claims and conclusions. The rule of logic states that because the expert finds the case to be true, and the expert is a valid source, then it is true. The precondition necessary to satisfy the use of this rule states that the claims presented in the body of evidence are based on reliable expert testimony relevant to the case defined by the research question. The strength and legitimacy of the argument are based on the expert testimony that created the discovery claims. Once the appropriate implicative logic has been determined, we can move on to Task 2.

TASK 2. REFRAME CLAIMS TO MEET THE PREREQUISITE CONDITIONS IDENTIFIED BY THE SELECTED LOGIC TYPE

Once we have identified the appropriate logic type and its prerequisites, we do the critique of the literature. This critique is an analysis of the claims and evidence of the discovery argument. The criteria for this analysis are the prerequisite conditions established by the logic type. The purpose of the analysis is to align or reframe discovery claims so they become valid premises for the argument of advocacy.

Return to the example about red state and blue state cultures. Knowing the prerequisite conditions require the state or national policies that cause the creation of red state and blue states cultures, we return to our survey of literature and critique all of the claims and evidence to ensure we have identified all causal policies. We cull out those claims that are not causal. After completing this task, we now organize the reframed claims into premises.

TASK 3. BUILD THE ADVOCACY ARGUMENT

If Tasks 1 and 2 have been done correctly, Task 3 becomes a simple exercise. Having the correct premises organized and defined and knowing the appropriate logic type makes drawing conclusions easy. These declarative statements will quickly become evident when we complete this statement: "Since these are the facts of the case, we can only conclude. . . ."

Let's return to the example about red and blue state cultures to examine how the advocacy argument can be made. Say we have identified 25 major national and state policies as the premises that caused the creation of red state and blue state cultures in the United States. Since our question asked us to determine what policies led up to the creation of this phenomenon, we simply have to organize, perhaps classify, these policies to construct the thesis statement to answer the research question posed by the study.

Building the Literature Review Case: An Example

Now let us examine how the entire literature review case is built. We continue with the example given in Chapter 4, "History of the Theory of Intelligence." A map of its argument for discovery appears in Figure 5.6. This map shows how a researcher was able to address the question, "What is the definition of human intelligence?"

When examining the far left column of Figure 5.6, notice that this researcher collected the various major theories on human intelligence by theoretical contributors. As seen in the center column of the figure, the theoretical perspectives fell within two camps when the researcher tallied the data to develop the body of evidence. The researcher used a complex warranting scheme, building arguments of side-by-side reasoning, to organize the simple claims into the evidence supporting each major theory. Divergent mapping shows two major theoretical camps in opposition. This complex reasoning scheme then became the warrant for asserting the claim that two prominent theoretical positions on the nature of human intelligence were held in the 20th century. The far right column of Figure 5.6 shows the major claim.

The major claim that was a product of the argument of discovery from the literature survey now becomes the premise used to develop the argument of advocacy. Figure 5.7 depicts how the second argument supports the thesis of the case.

When developing the argument of advocacy, the researcher stated the study question as originally framed as the study topic. The thesis of the literature review must address the question of what is the argument pattern type. In this example, the research question is, "What are the prominent postulated 20th-century theories addressing the nature of cognitive intelligence?" The thesis of this researcher's literature review

Figure 5.6   Theories of Intelligence: The Discovery Argument

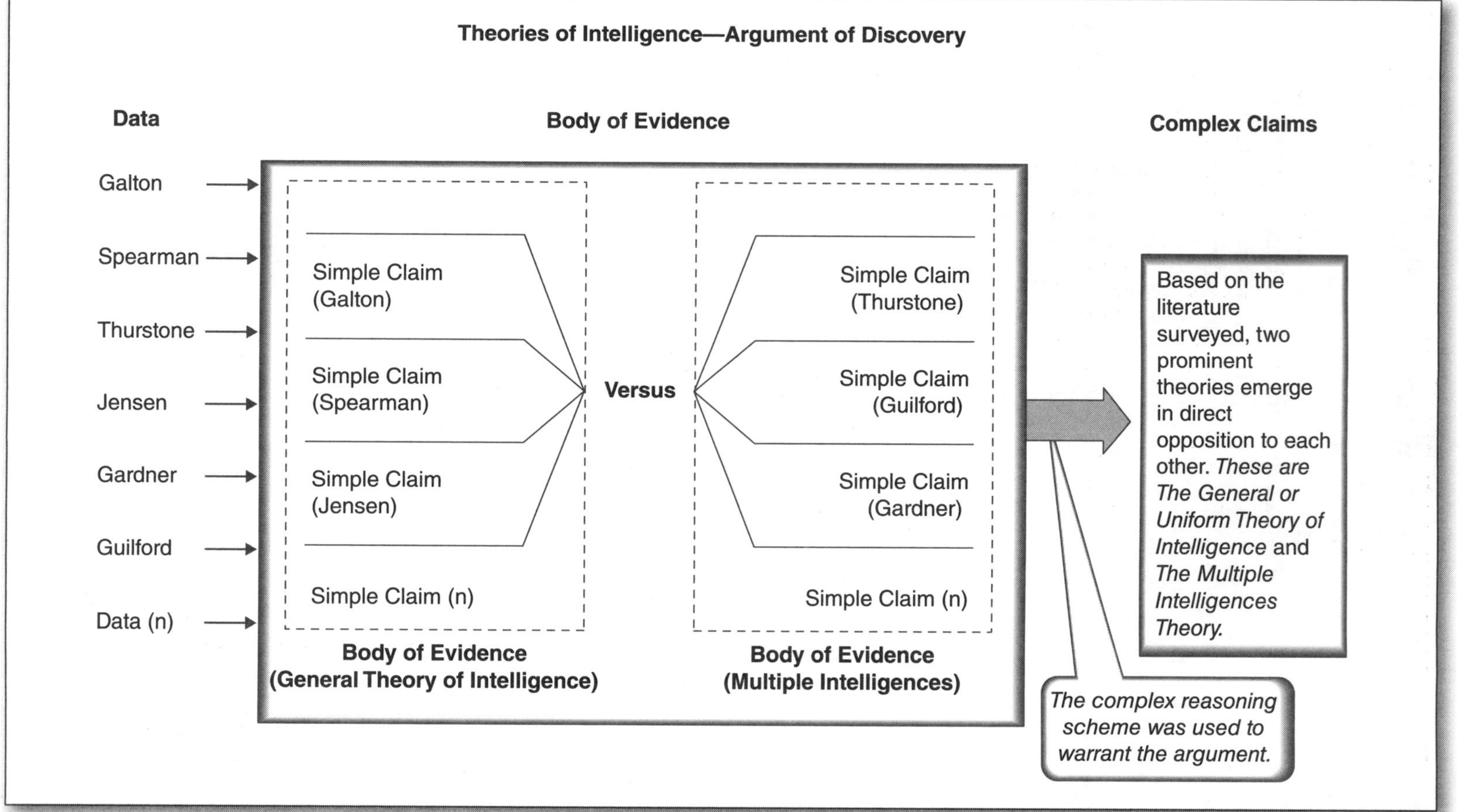

Theories of Intelligence—Argument of Discovery

Complex Claims

Data

Based on the literature surveyed, two prominent theories emerge in direct opposition to each other. *These are The General or Uniform Theory of Intelligence and The Multiple Intelligences Theory.*

The complex reasoning scheme was used to warrant the argument.

Body of Evidence

Galton
Spearman
Thurstone
Jensen
Gardner
Guilford
Data (n)

Simple Claim (Galton)
Simple Claim (Spearman)
Simple Claim (Jensen)
Simple Claim (n)

Body of Evidence
(General Theory of Intelligence)

Versus

Simple Claim (Thurstone)
Simple Claim (Guilford)
Simple Claim (Gardner)
Simple Claim (n)

Body of Evidence
(Multiple Intelligences)

Figure 5.7 Theories of Intelligence: The Advocacy Argument

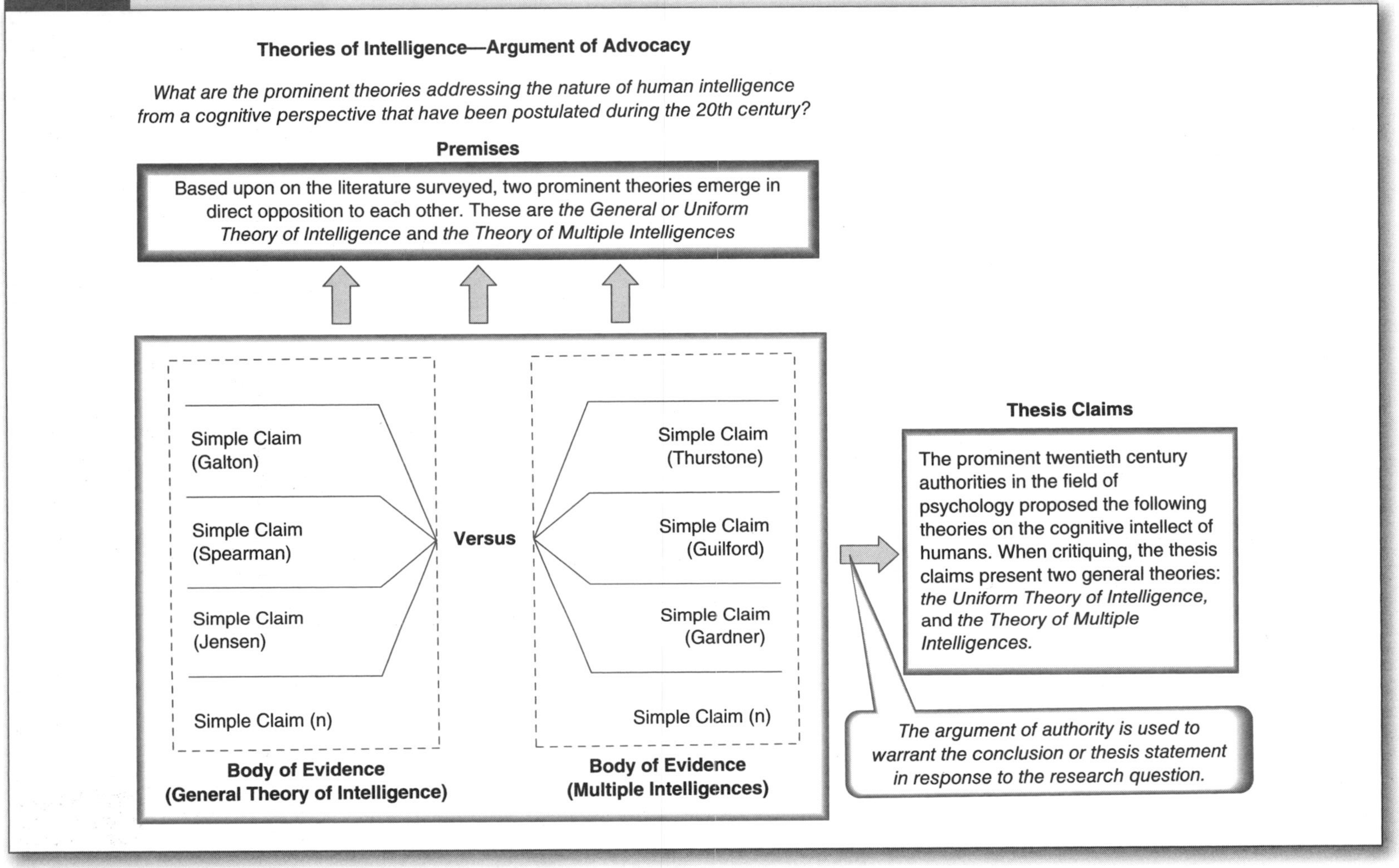

Theories of Intelligence—Argument of Advocacy

What are the prominent theories addressing the nature of human intelligence from a cognitive perspective that have been postulated during the 20th century?

Premises

Based upon on the literature surveyed, two prominent theories emerge in direct opposition to each other. These are *the General or Uniform Theory of Intelligence and the Theory of Multiple Intelligences*

Body of Evidence (General Theory of Intelligence)

Simple Claim (Galton)

Simple Claim (Spearman)

Simple Claim (Jensen)

Simple Claim (n)

Versus

Body of Evidence (Multiple Intelligences)

Simple Claim (Thurstone)

Simple Claim (Guilford)

Simple Claim (Gardner)

Simple Claim (n)

Thesis Claims

The prominent twentieth century authorities in the field of psychology proposed the following theories on the cognitive intellect of humans. When critiquing, the thesis claims present two general theories: *the Uniform Theory of Intelligence, and the Theory of Multiple Intelligences.*

The argument of authority is used to warrant the conclusion or thesis statement in response to the research question.

125

must answer this question. The researcher must assemble and argue the current understanding about the prominent cognitive theories dealing with human intelligence in a way that successfully answers the question. The argument pattern type is one of authority. This work begins by presenting what is known.

Beginning with the left-hand columns of Figure 5.7, the researcher transfers the claims made in the argument of discovery to the premises of the argument of advocacy. These claims are now the supporting evidence the researcher uses to make the argument in response to the study question. In the example, a synthesis of the premise states, "Based on the literature surveyed, two prominent theories emerge in direct opposition to each other. These are the general or uniform theory of intelligence and the theory of multiple intelligences." The data provided to support this premise are the evidence supplied by the simple claims presented in the argument of discovery.

At this point, the researcher has stated the current knowledge about the question posed. Do the premises stated answer the study question? When applying the premise to the study question, it becomes obvious there is a satisfactory response. Psychologists in the 20th century postulated two significant theories about the nature of human intelligence. Does this information properly respond to the study question? If so, which seems likely, the literature review presents evidence addressing the research question. However, is the claim or thesis statement warranted? What makes this evidence believable? Here, the researcher must review the divergent reasoning pattern (see Chapter 4) to justify the reliability and truth of the premises. At that point, the researcher can successfully argue that these premises are reliable and valid.

What logic allows the researcher to assert that because the various authors have claimed these theoretical principles, their testimony provides a justification for asserting the thesis? The researcher uses an implicative argument of *authority* to justify the thesis, as shown in the right-hand column of Figure 5.7. The researcher states the thesis: "The prominent 20th-century authorities in psychology proposed the following theories on the cognitive intellect of humans. When critiquing, the thesis claims present two general theories: the uniform theory of intelligence and the theory of multiple intelligences."

To make the implicative connection between the premises built in the argument of discovery, the researcher examined the nature of those premises and found them built on authoritative evidence. Reasoning from authority makes good sense because the body of evidence is well grounded by expert testimony. Thus, by using this argument pattern type as a warranting scheme, the argument of advocacy asserts a rational conclusion. However, the critique can continue further. Notice that evidence supporting the premise comes from divergent mapping. The researcher's responsibility is to present the rebuttal cases made by each of these opposing views to further explain and qualify the thesis statement. To complete the literature critique, the researcher must present the points and counterpoints of the debate. At the end of this evaluative discussion, the researcher might even decide that one of the theories is more convincing than the other. The researcher might also consider the possibility of extending the current knowledge about the research subject by developing a new research question that would suggest original research to provide an answer to the current debate.

EXERCISE 5.1

Evaluating the Literature Critique

Use the following steps to review your literature critique. Examine your own work to evaluate its strength.

1. Review your original study question. Do the premises built in Argument 1 provide a satisfactory answer to the research question? If not, what work do you need to do next? If the answer is satisfactory, then the premises lead directly to declaring the thesis.

2. Examine the nature of the evidence presented to support the premises in answering the study question. Is the evidence based on cause and effect, effect to cause, sign, sample to population, population to sample, parallel case, analogy, authority, or ends-means? Often more than one argument pattern type might fit. If so, select the argument pattern type that makes the most persuasive argument. Compose the thesis statement or research problem. Ensure that you have support for the case of the argument pattern type.

3. Build the critique discussion. In support of the thesis, analyze and evaluate the premises and body of evidence built in the argument of discovery to further clarify the key ideas offered by the thesis. For example, this critique could entail modeling key parts, an evaluation of the debate, a clarification of the omissions and gaps in the current knowledge, or the definitional development of the thesis.

CONCEPT 6. FALLACIES

Beware of the pitfall of fallacious arguments, or **fallacies**, which are arguments that lead to a mistaken or misleading conclusion. As seen earlier, a lack of convincing data, inappropriate or disconnected evidence, and unwarranted claims can all lead to a fallacious argument. The three most common fallacies in argumentation are jumping to conclusions, general-izations, and overlooking alternative explanations.

Here are some of the major fallacies researchers must avoid:

1. When a researcher asserts a conclusion based on skeletal evidence, the risk of *jumping to a faulty conclusion* increases. Building a falla-cious argument by jumping to a conclusion can also be caused by an incomplete evaluation of the evidence.

2. Another great temptation for the researcher is to bias the argument by *presenting a conclusion without properly addressing other alterna-tives.* Researchers rarely have a one-sided argument. When such a case seemingly presents itself, usually the researcher either was blinded by a preferred conclusion or did not delve deeply enough into the data to find alternative possibilities. Avoiding these temp-tations will help ensure research strength.

3. Research that engages in *name-calling* attacks data, a position taken, or an expert by impugning the personal character of the author. "Nothing my honored opponent says is trustworthy."

4. Research that appeals to *emotions* bases its argument on an emo-tional rather than an evidentiary position. It makes its appeal to the crowd or draws its conclusion based on groupthink rather than from building a rational case for its conclusion. "All good patriots must support my view."

5. Research that appeals to *ignorance* uses the logic that a claim must be true because it has not been proven false. This backdoor logic for proving the existence of a claim is simply wrong. "It's obvious to all of us that . . . ."

6. *Misplaced causality* often occurs when research uses the arguments of cause to effect or effect to cause. As shown earlier, to prove causality, you must ensure an irrefutable connection between the action and its effect. You must also show that the causes are solely responsible for those effects. Too many researchers argue causality without considering other actions or events that could have a bearing on the connection. "It's evident from the low test scores that teachers are incompetent."

7. Research that *begs the question* occurs when the researcher asserts a claim and uses that claim as the evidence for the assertion. This is circular reasoning. "There is a God because God said so."

8. Research that reaches a *disconnected conclusion* does so without evidence to support it. Either there is no evidence presented to back up the claim or there is no connection between the evidence

presented and the claim proposed. "We must invade Iraq because they have weapons of mass destruction."

9. Research that reaches an *"everybody knows that" conclusion* appears to make a case where none exists. Here, the researcher draws a conclusion based on some ill-defined or vague notion of a case. No evidence is presented—neither expert testimony nor observation. Instead, the researcher bases the claim on false premises or on opinion.

10. Research that results in a *loaded question* has formed a research question that contains one or more false or questionable presuppositions. The classic example is, "When did you stop beating your wife?" Notice that this question is fraught with presupposition. It assumes that you have a wife and that you beat her. These assumptions assume facts without the backing of any supporting evidence. The researcher commits this fallacy when composing a research question in which one or more of the key concepts depend on unproven presuppositions that propose a truth but that lack authentication.

11. Research that *poisons the well* biases the argument by using controlling language. Here, the researcher uses descriptive language to sell the argument, either negatively or positively, without respect for the evidence. "This study examined the effects that the bureaucratic, authoritarian, and wasteful No Child Left Behind Act had on the reading achievement of third-grade inner-city children in California."

There are many other fallacious arguments. The ones mentioned here are a few of the more common ones that you might meet. Remember, making strong arguments of discovery and advocacy are the best ways to avoid fallacious arguments.

CONCEPT 7. THE CASE IS EVERYTHING

The thesis case is the critical part of any literature review. Unless a literature review presents a sound case that backs up its thesis, it fails to meet its purpose and lacks any credibility. Presenting the case, the soundness of the case's arguments, and the clarity of the case's logic are the primary concerns of the literature survey and the literature critique. When building a literature survey and a literature critique, you must constantly decide whether you are making a case correctly. The thesis of any study is only as good as the case that supports it. As the Italian proverb puts it, *"Botte buona fa buon vino."*

Tips

1. Make sure the literature critique is forceful and defendable. It is the last impression left with your readers.

2. After your literature critique is complete, review the figures in Chapter 5 as a means of checking the case you have built.

3. Review your arguments to identify the reasoning patterns you have used. Do they meet the preconditions?

4. Check the list of fallacies to be certain that you have not fallen prey to any of them.

SUMMARY

This chapter explained how to create the argument of advocacy necessary to support the case for the literature review. It dealt with the purpose of a literature critique and the three activities necessary to complete this task. Using if/then logic as the foundation for the thesis, the chapter showed the connection between the discovery and advocacy arguments. The nine linking patterns provide avenues for building strong, implicative logic between the research study question and the premises that warrant the thesis of the study. A good literature critique must not only prove the advocacy argument, tying what is known to what can be concluded, but it must also provide the necessary evidence to describe fully the implications of that thesis. Finally, the chapter supplied a list of common fallacies that can become pitfalls of good argumentation.

CHECKLIST

Task	Completed
Reviewing the Topic Question	
1. Analyze the question framed as the basis of your study.	☐
2. Identify which implicative warrant type is inferred by the study question.	☐
Building the Advocacy Argument	
1. Build the premises from the complex claims of the discovery argument.	☐
2. Organize the premises with a suitable warrant scheme.	☐
3. Build the advocacy argument.	☐
4. Build the thesis statement.	☐

REFLECTIVE OVERSIGHT

1. Have I successfully identified which warrant type provides the logic for answering the topic question?

2. Do I have a convincing advocacy argument to support the thesis of the study?

Step 6. Write the Review

📖 **Task 1.** Write to Understand

- ○ *Activity 1. Review Notes and Memoranda*
- ○ *Activity 2. Exploratory Write*
- ○ *Activity 3. Outline*
- ○ *Activity 4. Write Preliminary Draft*

📖 **Task 2.** Write to Be Understood

- ○ *Activity 1. Write the First Draft*
- ○ *Activity 2. Revise—Working the Second and Third Drafts*
- ○ *Activity 3. Complete the Final Draft*

📖 **Submit the Literature Review**

6

Step Six: Write the Review

Write, Audit, Edit

Scribendi recte sapere est principium et fons.
The secret of all good writing is sound judgment.

—Horace

The Literature Review Model

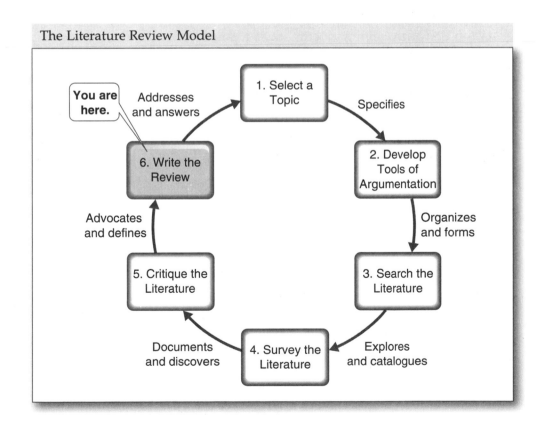

KEY VOCABULARY

- **Auditing**—Reviewing completed work to check and align content and to proofread.

- **Writing to Understand**—Journals, memoranda, notes, outlines, and all other forms of writing that allow the researcher to internalize the data, evidence, and arguments to be used in the literature review.

- **Writing to Be Understood**—The preliminary, first, and subsequent drafts of a work that give the reader a complete and convincing understanding of the researcher's thesis.

The research critique is complete, and a research case has been developed. The background information is organized and mapped, and the evidence is cataloged and documented. You have interpreted, analyzed, and developed arguments, written memoranda, completed a project journal, taken notes, and done some exploratory writing. All of the pieces are at your fingertips. The task is simple now . . . or is it? Some students believe all they need to do is assemble the research information and begin typing, but formal writing does not begin with composing the first draft. Far from it.

Applying a critical-thinking step to the literature review process suggests the literature review document is a communication device serving two functions. First, its contents provide new knowledge to be added to the current understanding about the topic. Second, its contents document the case and the case's thesis conclusion for independent review and verification. A literature review is not merely a book report; it is much more. The literature review document is a formal presentation, a written synthesis of the case and the conclusions drawn. It is writing for a specific purpose. In his book, *The New Writing with a Purpose* (2014), Joseph Trimmer calls it *writing research*, specifically *writing the argument*. As such, the production of this document requires a specific writing strategy. The writer uses an expository writing strategy to accomplish the objective: to develop and compose the case and thesis. You have defined the subject of study, collected the relevant data, patterned the evidence, and built a justifiable case supporting the thesis conclusion. Now it is time to compose.

Academic composition requires you to deliberately create, mold, and refine the case. It starts with imagining how your end product will look. Then, through many revisions, which involve composing, auditing, and editing, the work evolves into a final polished product. The finished document requires completing two tasks. During Task 1, the writer is writing to understand. During Task 2, the author is writing to be understood (Figure 6.1). First, write to learn what needs to be said, and then write to learn how to say it to an audience. The purpose of this chapter is to explain these tasks.

THE WRITING PROCESS: OVERVIEW

Each writing task includes activities that develop and refine the work, resulting in a final draft suitable for publishing. The subsequent list summarizes the necessary activities for these two tasks. The tasks are explained in detail later in the chapter.

Figure 6.1	The Writing Process

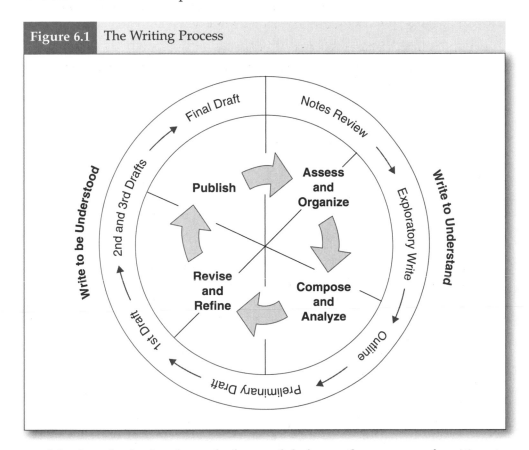

Moving clockwise through the model shows the process of writing to understand. Start by assessing and organizing the subject matter of the composition. Reviewing notes and memoranda developed in the survey and critique of the literature bring the subject matter into focus. An initial draft, called the exploratory write, crystallizes and assesses your internalized knowledge about the subject, providing the foundations for the eventual composition. An annotated outline is built to sequence and form the subject matter for composition. Using the results of the exploratory write and the annotated outline, the preliminary draft is then crafted. This draft is the first full-scale rendition of the work. Once edited for accuracy, continuity, structure, and grammar, the preliminary draft is then refined into a first draft.

The first draft is the initial attempt to write for a specific audience—writing to be understood. The second and all subsequent drafts are composed based on audits and feedback from outside experts, continuing the process of composition refinement. Once all changes have been made to the work based upon previous drafts, the final, or published, draft is composed. This draft incorporates all the revisions to content, structure, grammar, and composition.

Good writing comes from constant editing and revision. No matter which draft you are working on, the process is the same. You first write, then audit to find errors and omissions, then edit to correct and revise the work (Figure 6.2).

This process always begins with writing, be it an outline, a first draft, or a final draft. After writing comes **auditing**, which is an inspection of the recently completed work. When auditing an outline or draft, check and align the content and proofread it carefully. The purpose of the audit is twofold. It must uncover all flaws in the work and assess the success of the draft in meeting its intent.

When editing, adjust the content and flow of the composition and correct its organization and grammar. Remember that using software programs to do grammar and spell checks is not the same as proofreading the work yourself. The product of the edit is a revision of the previous composition. Writing, auditing, and editing continue throughout the writing process, refining the work until the project is completed.

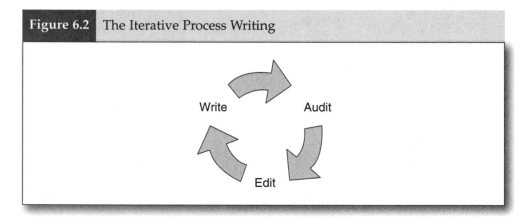

| Figure 6.2 | The Iterative Process Writing |

TASK 1. WRITE TO UNDERSTAND

Writing to understand is a formative act of learning and owning the subject matter. First, gather and organize the ideas that make up the research content. You must assimilate, arrange, and form these ideas into a framework for composition. The act of composing begins with summing up and transforming the threads of data into a new, original, cohesive expression of those data. You must create the pattern of the story, weaving the threads of each idea together to form the composition. Only you can do this. Remember the example of the jigsaw puzzle? When assembling the puzzle, the puzzle maker looks at the picture on the box to see how the pieces fit together. A writer, too, must see a picture of the subject matter to begin writing. If this mental image is not created, the writing will not form. So how is this image created?

Activity 1. Reviewing Notes and Memoranda

Your memoranda (a collection of informal directive, advisory, and informative writing), your daily progress and ideas journal, and your notes will all act as reminders of past work. Throughout the survey and critique of the literature, you have chronicled your ideas as a prelude to formal writing. Reviewing these preliminary thoughts now will assist in the process of internalizing the data you have worked so hard to gather. Assimilating the subject matter into personal understanding begins with subject comprehension. Working with notes and memoranda creates an understanding of the subject matter, which facilitates the emergence of original ideas and knowledge patterns. These patterned images create a new meaning that becomes the foundation of the initial written composition.

Activity 2. Exploratory Writing

Creating Writing Readiness

Researchers are outside observers when conducting research. Gathering data, identifying evidence, and building a case are all exercises in working with others' ideas. While personal knowledge of the subject grows throughout the research work and attendant note taking, it is still recall and remains abstract, disjointed, and untested. The writer is dependent on notes, memoranda, a journal, outlines, and maps. This subject material must be internalized. You cannot remain the outsider noting and recording ideas; you must now become the critical insider creating and composing new meaning.

To have command of the subject knowledge, you must study the material as if you were preparing for a final exam. Pretend you are going to teach this material to a group of students. Do you know it well enough to teach it to others? Is it organized in your mind? Can you anticipate questions about the material? If the answer to any of these questions is no, you need to spend more time on preparation.

Most writers know that writing is the great arbiter of their knowledge. They cannot write what they do not know. When beginning to write, this fact becomes painfully clear. To write successfully on any topic, you must learn it so thoroughly that it becomes a familiar friend. Unless you first thoroughly learn the material, you are trying to sew a garment with thread but no fabric.

Ask yourself two questions:

1.   What do I actually know about my subject?

2.   How will I explain it to someone else?

Exploratory composition provides the opportunity to test your familiarity with, and understanding of, the research. Without the aid of support or background material, write what you know about your research. The following is a guided exercise in this necessary step. An exploratory write is done from memory after reviewing your initial notes. A review of the notes will provide the recall necessary to tackle the exploratory write with confidence and clarity.

EXERCISE 6.1

Guided Exercise for Exploratory Composition

Directions: This composition should come from the top of your head. Do not use any notes or supporting materials. Write a paper of no more than five pages responding to the following questions.

1. What is your topic?

2. What do you know about the topic?

3. What is the context or background surrounding the topic?

4. How is this topic significant?

5. What is your central claim or thesis?

6. How can you prove it?

7. What conclusions have you drawn, and what reasons support them?

8. What are the implications of your research for the academic field?

When you have completed this paper, put it down and leave it for several days. After returning to the paper, check your readiness for writing a literature review. Use the following audit questions to discover your familiarity with the subject. If you need to review the materials, refer to the chapters as noted.

1. Have you accurately defined the topic and its core concepts? (Chapter 1)

2. Is the topic clear and concise? (Chapter 1)

3. Have you described the general issue or concern that inspired the topic? (Chapter 1)

4. Have you identified the academic area of your approach, and is your language recognizably the language used in that academic field? (Chapter 1)

5. Does this topic clarify your original interest? How does the topic respond to the interest? (Chapter 1)

6. Does your evidence show that this study is important to the field? (Chapter 1)

7. Do you have a sound argument of discovery for what is known about the topic? (Chapters 2 and 4)

8. How does the argument of advocacy address the problem? (Chapter 5)

9. What is the proof or evidence for your thesis? (Chapter 5)

10. Based on your thesis, do your conclusions resolve the problem or question prompted by your first interest? (Chapter 5)

11. Do your conclusions and your arguments work as a unified case—a compelling whole? (Chapter 5)

After studying your guided writing and the audit question responses, what more do you need to know about your topic? This is an opportunity to take stock of your efforts and to decide whether it is time to move forward or if you first need to go back and gather more information to build a better personal understanding of the research case.

Activity 3. Outlining

The audit of the exploratory composition can create an immediate compulsion to write. Resist this urge. The ideas, threads, and patterns that emerged from your exploratory composition must first be arranged into a well-organized, cohesive, and complete body of knowledge. You must ensure that all the pieces of the puzzle are present and in their correct places. This is a time for analysis and reflection. Producing an annotated outline allows you to carry out this necessary task.

Outlining, the third task in writing to understand, is the tried-and-true method for beginning the formal development of the composition. The outline serves as an organizer that documents your thinking about the research. Here you wed the personal intent and perspective created in the exploratory write to your researched information to form a comprehensive profile of the subject. Outlining serves three purposes: It acts as (1) a mechanism for integrating and transforming ideas, (2) a mechanism of sequencing those ideas, and (3) a general plan for the composition.

The outline provides an integrating mechanism. When outlining, you are constantly moving subject knowledge from a cursory understanding of another's work to an intimate personal understanding of the subject. The necessary reflective thinking forces you to shift from collecting and reporting ideas to knowing those ideas, analyzing them, and interpreting them. Thinking through an outline transforms your perspective from observer of information to the author of a literature review.

Outlining also acts as a sequencing mechanism. When forming the outline, you must organize information, arrange ideas, and create the threads and patterns for the composition. You must articulate concrete ideas, place these ideas into logical sequences, and build logical patterns to combine these sequences into cohesive patterns of thought. An outline constantly demands that you reflect on what information has come before, what information is currently being included, and what information logically comes next. The outline is a record of the idea sequence and the road map for writing.

Finally, the outline is the general plan for the literature review composition. It sketches the overall design and notes the essential features of the work. Think of an outline as the blueprint for a house you are building. The outline provides a design plan for the written composition. It both clarifies the big picture and provides the specific dimensions for each of the parts or sections of the written work.

Review the completed outline for specificity. Does it provide clear direction and enough information to allow you to advance with a minimum of second-guessing and rethinking? Does it provide a sound overall design? Does it include all the details necessary to support developing the design?

The first step in building an outline is to create a table of contents. The table of contents becomes a frame for the composition by laying out the major sections of the work in a logical fashion. If a format template, which includes a table of contents, has been provided, use it. Be aware that in general, the three major parts for the literature review are the introduction, the body, and the summation.

Once you complete the outline, you should leave it for a day or two. After suitable time for reflection, thoroughly review the outline to ensure that it is complete, properly sequenced, and clear enough to provide a map for written composition. The following questions can help guide this stage of your review:

1. Does the outline flow from one main idea to the next in a reasoned fashion?

2. Does it thoroughly capture the contents?

3. Are the claims made supported by strong evidence?

4. Are all the conclusions warranted?

5. Do the thesis points flow logically from one to the next?

6. Does the outline represent an integrated whole?

7. Have you omitted all incorrect or repetitious information items?

Rework the outline until you can answer each of these questions affirmatively. Proofread your work. Review it not only for errors but also for its depth, connectivity, and continuity. Make the necessary corrections and be alert for any mistakes.

Some Common Outlining Mistakes

To make your outline as useful as possible, avoid the following common errors:

- Resist the urge to compile just a list of facts and ideas. Listing quotes and ideas randomly is easy to do. While such a list might provide relevant details, it cannot provide the connections and theme for the written work. A list does not project the overall picture.
- Include all the pertinent information by doing research. Failure to include all the relevant ideas will result in an incomplete outline, which can only lead to an incomplete composition.
- Avoid writer overconfidence, or overreliance on personal retention of the subject matter, which can result in an outline that is either too brief or too vague. In this case, the outline does not provide enough descriptive detail to provide a clear understanding of the material. A brief or vague outline lacks queuing specificity.
- Do not consider the outline a shorthand version of the preliminary draft. There is a tendency to include too much information when writing an outline. This will produce too many fine details, which will soon obscure the big picture. Remember, the outline builds the blueprint, not the house.

How can you avoid these mistakes? Remember, the outline should provide the directions for writing the document. When building the outline, ensure that all the information is assembled. Refer back to the memoranda and the journal you developed along the way. Spend time reflecting on your material so you can produce the cognitive structures and content themes necessary to build the story line.

Literature Review Format

The *introduction* to the literature review provides a profile of the study. Its purpose is to engage the reader by presenting highlights of the essential parts of the work. The *body* presents the case and documents it to justify the research thesis. Finally, the *summation* gives a summary of the research study's conclusions. The introduction, the body, and the summation are divided into subject sections.

The Introduction: There are six sections to be outlined in the introduction: (1) the opening, (2) the study topic, (3) the context, (4) the significance, (5) the problem statement, and (6) the organization.

The *opening* draws the reader into the work. It can be a poignant example, the essence of a debate on the question, or the question posed by the study. A narrative hook to grab the reader's attention may encourage the reader to continue reading by playing on emotions, attitudes, or beliefs. Consider this example: "Local school boards have abandoned the constituencies that put them in office. They have elected instead to become cogs in the wheels of state bureaucracies. Today, school boards are simply apparatchiks of the state." This example contains three powerful claims. These claims aim to elicit an emotional response from the reader that should create a continued interest in reading the work.

The *topic section* should be a concise statement identifying the key ideas of the research. It should state the focus and perspective taken in addressing the topic. It should also clearly define each of the key ideas within the topic section. The topic section should be no more than two or three paragraphs in length.

The *context section* addresses the study's setting. It recounts the circumstances that surround, and perhaps have created, the research problem, such as academic debates or concerns. The circumstances could also be practical issues or problems that have led to studying the problem. The context section should provide information that defines the research problem's environment.

The *significance*, or needs statement, provides the justification for the study. This section recounts the writer's personal interest in the subject of study and provides documentation justifying the study's value to the academic community. The value of the research study should address the importance of solving the practical problem or why an academic issue needs clarification or resolution.

The *problem statement*, or thesis question, is the question that needs to be answered by the research study. This statement must be presented in a clear and concise manner in no more than two or three sentences. The problem statement can be followed by two or three paragraphs of explanation.

The introduction ends with an *organization section* that provides the reader with a framework stating how the literature review will be presented.

The Body: The body of the literature review presents the case for the thesis in two sections, the background research of the study and the study's conclusion. The *background* of the study tells the story. Here you present the arguments made for what is known about the topic of study. The literature survey tally matrix and the argument of discovery (Figure 6.3) serve as the major references for building the background section. These aids are foundation resources. They document and catalog the claim statements, supporting evidence, suitable citations, and warrant justification necessary to build the argument for what is known. Use these reference aids as organizers to develop the background statement. The reasoning pattern made for the argument of discovery becomes the profile for the story line for writing the body. The major parts of the reasoning pattern become the headings and subheadings of this section of the literature review.

The information contained in the literature survey tally matrix provides the necessary data to build the details into the story line. The background of the study is derived from the discovery argument. The purpose of this section is to present what is known about the topic of study. This section is a product of the literature survey and the literature critique.

The study's conclusion section is taken from the advocacy argument. Here you present the thesis case. You present the claims, evidence, and justification of the argument leading to the thesis.

The second activity develops the thesis argument. Using the conclusions of the background statement as the starting point, state the implications of what is known to address the research problem. The literature critique developed the contents for this section.

Figure 6.3 Major Reference Aids

	Stage 1. Assemble the collected data.				Stage 2. Organize the information.				Stage 3. Analyze the patterns of data.		
	Key concept or descriptor (1)	Citation or reference (2)	Main ideas (3)	Data quality (4)	Evidence categories (5)	Warrant scheme and simple arguments (6)	Simple claim statement (7)	Claim acceptability (8)	Simple claim statement (premises) (9)	Warrant scheme and complex argument (10)	Complex claim statement (11)
	Taken from maps and bibliographic entry card	Taken from maps and bibliographic entry card	Taken from maps and bibliographic entry card	Do data meet quality standards? (yes or no)	Data entry placement into a body of evidence	Warrant scheme used for this evidence group	Data entry is evidence for this claim	Does claim meet acceptability standards? (yes or no)	Simple claim placement as an evidence statement for the major claim	Warrant scheme used to justify the complex argument	The thesis for the discovery argument
Author Text Periodical (A)											
Author Text Periodical (B)											
Author Text Periodical (C)											
Author Text Periodical (n)											

Survey of Literature
Argument of Discovery

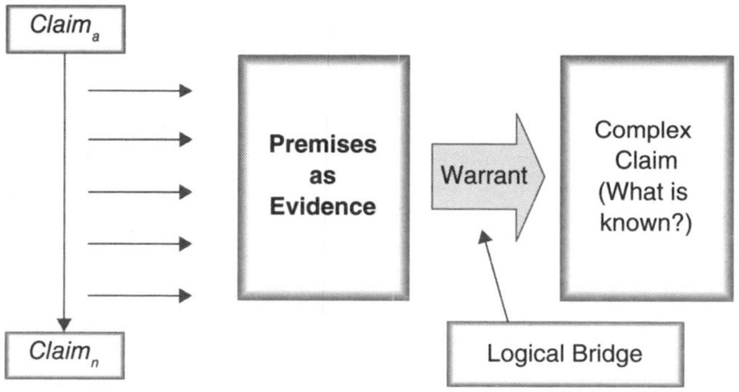

$Claim_a$

$Claim_n$

Premises as Evidence

Warrant

Complex Claim (What is known?)

Logical Bridge

Given the data on the subject, this is what we know . . .

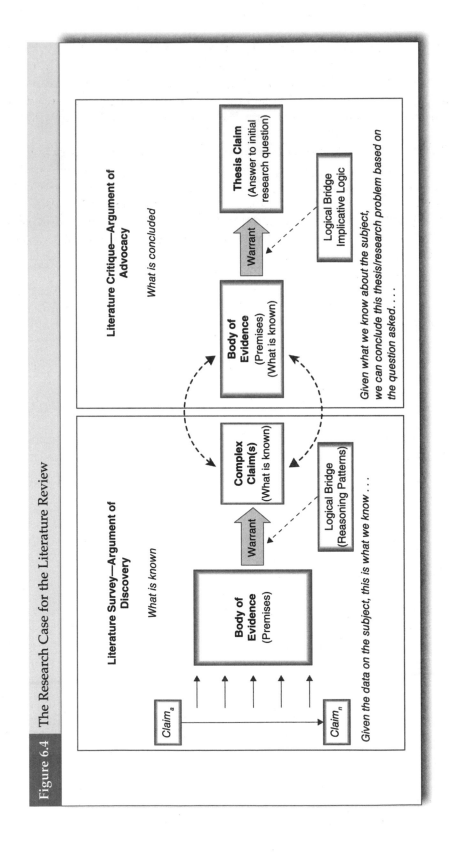

Figure 6.4   The Research Case for the Literature Review

Literature Critique—Argument of Advocacy

What is concluded

Thesis Claim
(Answer to initial research question)

Warrant

Logical Bridge
Implicative Logic

Body of Evidence
(Premises)
(What is known)

*Given what we know about the subject,
we can conclude this thesis/research problem based on
the question asked. . . .*

Literature Survey—Argument of Discovery

What is known

Complex Claim(s)
(What is known)

Warrant

Logical Bridge
(Reasoning Patterns)

Body of Evidence
(Premises)

Claim$_a$

Claim$_n$

Given the data on the subject, this is what we know . . .

Use the literature survey tally matrix and the research case for the literature review model (Figure 6.4) as the references for developing the thesis argument. The implicative logic pattern used to justify the thesis argument is the basis of the story line. Again, the major claim, supporting simple claims, evidence, and citations can provide the details for this section of the body of the review.

The Summation: This section of the literature review summarizes the thesis argument. It is made up of the thesis statement, the thesis analysis, and the study's implications.

The summation section begins by restating the research thesis. Next, the analysis provides a detailed interpretation and explanation of the thesis. Here you can note an explanation of the key ideas of the thesis, provide further definition to those ideas, and explore the thesis from various perspectives. Finally, the implications state the impact of the thesis on the practical everyday issue or academic question that motivated the research study. In this section, you note how the thesis solves the problem of the study.

Figure 6.5 shows the major parts and sections of a literature review. It also provides a listing of the study aids, maps, and references that can help build a review. The chapter references are listed for the reader's convenience.

Composing Drafts

Writing a literature review requires the creation of a series of drafts until the final composition emerges. Many years ago, a close friend of ours, Tim Cahill, then an aspiring young author, casually reflected about his writing:

> Writing is a lot like having a baby. You go through months of pregnancy. The baby grows. You experience frustration and elation, depression and expectation. There is labor. You work hard. The baby is born. I feel like I am pregnant when I write.

Writing is the conception, gestation, and maturation of an idea. First, ideas must be conceived and brought to the page. Once they arrive, they must be formed into something that will communicate with the reader. They must be molded and polished to create the written representation of what had been imagined by the mind's eye.

The vehicle that carries you through this transformation is the draft. Drafts are not just rewrites. They are a series of documents that evolve from first formation to final rendition. Drafts are stepping-stones that bridge the gap from beginning Task 1 (writing to understand) to completing Task 2 (writing to be understood).

Each draft has a specific purpose. These phases have rules of engagement, whether they are rules of composition, or grammar, or syntax. The

Figure 6.5   The Literature Review Outline: Study Aids, Maps, and References

The Literature Review Outline: Study Aids, Maps, or References		
Introduction Section of the Literature Review		
Subsection	**Study Aids, Maps, or References**	**Chapter**
Introductory statement	Narrative hook	Chapter 6
Study topic statement	The first library visit exercise	Chapter 1
Context statement	Defining a specific research interest	Chapter 1
Significance statement	Survey of literature, argument of discovery model	Chapter 4
	Literature survey tally matrix	Chapter 5
	Mapping schemes	Chapters 4 and 5
	Reasoning patterns	Chapters 4 and 5
	Literature critique advocacy model	Chapter 5
Problem statement	Survey of literature, argument of discovery model	Chapter 4
	Literature survey tally matrix	Chapter 5
	Mapping schemes	Chapters 4 and 5
	Reasoning patterns	Chapters 4 and 5
	Literature critique advocacy model	Chapter 5
Organization statement	The exploratory write	Chapter 6
Body Section of the Literature Review		
Subsection	**Study Aids, Maps, or References**	**Chapter**
Background section presenting current understanding of the topic (discovery argument used here)	Mapping schemes	Chapter 4
	Reasoning patterns	
	Survey of literature—Argument of discovery model	
	Literature survey tally matrix	
	Argument patterns	
Conclusions section presenting findings and conclusions that argue the thesis (advocacy argument used here)	Literature critique advocacy model	Chapter 5
	Research case of a literature review model	

Summation Section of the Literature Review		
Subsection	**Study Aids, Maps, or References**	**Chapter**
Thesis statement	Research case of a literature review model	Chapter 5
Thesis analysis	Research case of a literature review model, literature survey tally matrix	Chapters 4 and 5
Study implications	Defining a specific research interest	Chapter 1
	Research case of a literature review model	Chapter 5

phases are sequential to allow the writing to flow and to mature. As you move from one draft to the next, revise the writing. Drafting the work means revision that creates, molds, and finishes the written piece. When beginning to write, consider these suggestions:

- Reserve a quiet place for uninterrupted writing. Have comfort foods available if you need them, but don't make the writing place so comfortable that you become sleepy.
- Ensure that you have writing reference and support materials on hand, including an authoritative thesaurus and dictionary. Microsoft Word also provides a digital review tab, which includes a dictionary and a thesaurus. Often, the essence of a word or the synonym of a word will escape you as you write. These reference aids will help you to get the right idea on paper.
- Ensure that you have a significant block of time to get into the work so ideas flow. Good writing cannot be done in 15-minute spurts. Do not think about blocks of times in minutes, but in hours and days.
- Find your ideal time for writing. Is it in the early morning, or the late evening? Each of us has a time of day that lends itself to our best writing production. For many it is the early morning, when the mind is fresh and rested and there are fewer interruptions. Develop a regular schedule for your writing. A regular schedule will allow you to maintain the flow and pace of the writing.
- Schedule periodic breaks within your writing session. Give yourself time to stretch and reenergize, then return to work refreshed.
- Set a minimum page count as a goal and achieve that goal. Concentrate on writing each idea and producing the text.
- Have a plan about what you will write during the session. Create a mental picture of the piece. See its main ideas and its details.

Activity 4. Preliminary Drafting

Outlining organizes your thinking. Next, you must expand the outline into coherent sentences, complete paragraphs, and a cohesive composition. The preliminary draft is the first test of your true understanding of the material. What do you actually know about the subject? Can you express that knowledge in writing? Answering these questions is the task of a preliminary draft. This draft is the first attempt at narrating concrete statements in sequence.

The strategy for creating the preliminary draft will vary depending on your writing ability and content knowledge. Use the recommended strategy for framing any draft: write, audit, and edit. When composing a draft, first write it based on the intent and purpose of the draft. Next, audit the writing for content, sequence, composition, grammar, and cohesiveness. Finally, edit to fill in gaps and correct mistakes.

The preliminary draft has three major objectives. It allows you to (1) determine how to write the story, (2) transfer the early mental model of the subject into a concrete composition, and (3) check your knowledge of the subject.

Writing the preliminary draft may seem daunting. Take it one idea at a time, building each idea into paragraphs. Use the outline to decide how to arrange the writing. Choose a section and begin writing. When engaged in the preliminary write, write everything you know about that section or topic. The ideas will transform themselves as they leave the abstract and take the concrete form of the written word. Ideas will flow in randomly and in spurts. Try to order them while keeping the flow of the writing. Work at being concrete and sequential in your thinking. Take time to form the ideas and give them definition and clarity. Do not overthink or overwork an idea at the expense of losing the next idea. Remember, you will have the chance to polish your work later when you audit it.

Are you unsure of a word or idea? Refer to the dictionary. Dictionary definitions can help clear up mental blocks and ambiguity and provide the correct wording. Are you searching for the right word to express an idea? Use your thesaurus and look for synonyms. Are you unsure of what comes next? Play, scratch, doodle, or put words on paper. Eventually, the next idea will show up. If not, step away from the writing, take a break, and get some fresh air.

Preliminary Draft: The Audit

The purpose of this audit is twofold. It aligns your first rendition of the work with the subject outline. Second, it exposes any problems in content and composition that need attention. The steps used to audit the preliminary draft follow:

1. Before auditing the draft, allow at least 2 to 3 days, or preferably a week, to pass. This time enables the mind to erase the mental picture formed when writing the draft and will allow you to see the work with fresh eyes and an open mind. You will be surprised at what appears: dangling ideas, misplaced thoughts, sentences without meaning, vague language, and lapses in logic. What you thought was a good piece of work may reappear as a primitive work in progress.

2. Begin the draft by triple-spacing the work to allow room for additions and notes. Next, print it out. Viewing things on a computer screen allows you to see what you intended to write. Reading in a second format helps you pick up missed errors. Next, read the work aloud. Hear the words and thoughts as if you were encountering them for the first time. Note any incongruities, redundancies, and omissions.

3. As you read, audit the content of the work. Check for a consistent flow of ideas. Look for gaps in logic and knowledge. Review for the correct sequence of ideas. Ensure that proper transitions link major thoughts. Make sure that each paragraph has a beginning, middle, and an end. Finally, insert corrections where needed to cite evidence.

4. Once the content audit is complete, do a separate audit for grammar, composition, and style. Look for misused words and phrases. Check punctuation and spelling. Check for continuity of person, the use of active voice, and word economy. Again, correct any errors as you go. The seminal reference used to guide this step of the audit is *The Elements of Style* by Strunk and White (2000).

5. Complete the preliminary audit by aligning the draft to the subject outline. Place the written outline and the corrected draft side by side. Track the outline contents to reconcile the two. What needs adding, removing, or clarifying in the draft? You may need to refer to the tally matrix or other research references to align the draft. Make any necessary changes. Now is the time to insert the needed citations. Use the format style required by your academic discipline. All word processing programs and many digital reference aids include citation formatting for the most commonly used forms of classic footnotes or endnotes.

6. When you finish the audit, reread for a global view of the work. Check for content integrity and logic. Look for incomplete ideas. Ensure that you make suitable transitions. Double-check the order and the sequence of ideas.

Preliminary Draft: The Edit

After the audit is complete, it is time to revise. Use the marked-up copy of the draft created by the audit to rewrite the work. Make the line-by-line changes you noted. As you make changes, reread each sentence or paragraph for correctness and clarity before going on to the next. Continue until you finish the entire draft. Read the revision aloud to ensure that everything is in place. The ear will pick up errors and bumpy spots that the eye missed. Reading your writing silently allows your mind to substitute what you meant to say for what is actually on the page. Make any corrections needed.

The edit of the preliminary draft completes the transfer of subject knowledge to your consciousness. You now own the subject matter. The audit of the preliminary draft has forced you to develop the subject ideas into an original body of work. By auditing and editing the composition, you have cleanly penned it to paper. One question remains: Is the work understandable to others?

TASK 2. WRITE TO BE UNDERSTOOD

Writing to be understood is the act of drafting and redrafting the work into a finished piece that accurately and adequately communicates the subject ideas to others. Does the composition tell the story as you intended? Have you told the right story? Is the story told being heard? You are now writing for an audience. Essential to this undertaking is collaboration with others in the crafting of the work. Discussion with others about the form and content of the work provides the direction for each revision. Your thesis adviser, members of your study group, and friends can all help with this process. Based on the issues uncovered by each outside review, you can refine the work to increase clarity, continuity, and content integrity.

Each draft further develops the work and should make the picture more complete, more consistent in flow and voice, and more accurate in depicting the subject. You should ask, "Does the reader see what I see? If not, what must I change to bring the picture into focus?" With each revision, you should select readers to review the newest draft so you can use their responses for further editing.

Activity 1. Writing the First Draft

The preliminary draft provides a strong foundation for building a first draft. The focus of the first draft is to produce a clear, written communication and to increase audience understanding. To ensure that the best rendition of the work goes to others to review, complete one last reading of the first draft and check to ensure the following:

- Are syntax, voice, and paragraphing in alignment?
- Is the grammar correct?
- Is the piece written in active voice?
- Is the point of view consistent (first or third person)?
- Are verb tenses consistent (present or past)?
- Are paragraphs well formed and aligned?
- Have you followed your style manual?

STYLE MANUALS

A literature review is a formal document. Specific rules of style dictate its publication form and format. Recently, we found more than 150 style manuals that guide the formal publication of research works in the United States. Each academic field has its particular presentation format. The use of these manuals can vary by university, school, department, or even classroom instructor or research chair. Turabian, APA, and MLA are the most widely used in the social sciences in the United States. Become familiar with the style manual required for your research project. Take the time to examine your required manual for a general understanding of the rules of publication. Know how you will format, organize, and write your project. Each manual has specific rules for these issues.

A style manual, whether digital or hard copy, usually has the following sections:

- *The parts of the manuscript.* This section provides specific instructions about the front and back matter of your project. The information included specifies the format of your title page, copyright page, dedication or acknowledgment page, table of contents, and illustrations, among others.
- *Text composition.* This section provides instruction about the style of your work. The rules for punctuation, spelling, use of numbers, quotations, captions and legends, tables, bibliographies, and references are explained.
- *Rules for production.* This last section provides guidance on the formatting and form of the manuscript. The rules for formatting, pagination, headings, graphics, indent, and the production of figures and tables are found here.

The style manual is a reference work. After taking time to familiarize yourself with it, you will rely on it throughout the auditing and editing processes. When writing your preliminary draft, refer to your manual to set the correct format (font, margins, and so on) for the manuscript. When auditing the preliminary draft, ensure the text composition conforms to your style manual's directives. Audit the style again when you are preparing your first draft for outside review. To ensure that you are following the rules for publishing, refer to the style manual as necessary as you audit each successive draft. Finally, conduct a style audit for the last edit before formal publication

Double-check for accuracy and strength of evidence and the integrity of the case you are arguing. In *The Logic of Real Arguments* (2003), Alec Fisher suggests an easy way to check the integrity of arguments you have developed to make the thesis case of the work. The following exercise is based on this method. You might find it helpful in preparing the first draft. Have your notes, journal, memoranda, outline, logic maps, and tally matrix available for this exercise. They provide the necessary information for a quick alignment of the logic sequences.

This exercise provides a sound tool for analyzing and evaluating your research arguments. It should show the integrity of the arguments and provide an overall assessment of the quality of the research thesis. Identify the specific areas of strength and weakness in your research and correct them as needed. Once you have finished the first draft, it is time to send it out for auditing.

EXERCISE 6.2

Analyzing the Research Arguments and Case

The purpose here is critical analysis of the research arguments that make up the thesis case. You will identify all the parts of the research case and evaluate them to decide the validity of the research thesis. Analysis and evaluation are your two major tasks. First, analyze your work to check that the following conditions have been met:

- The main conclusions of the research are clear.
- The claims and evidence that support each conclusion are in place.
- The form and logic of each argument are stated or clearly implied.
- Each argument is warranted.

Second, evaluate the work to decide if the following are true:

- The logical reasoning is defendable.
- Suitable warranting supports the arguments' conclusions.
- The overall argumentation makes the thesis case.
- The correct style manual is followed.

First Draft: Analysis

1. Review the paper and look for the claim statements. *Underline them.*

2. Review the paper again and look for evidence statements. *Circle them.*

3. Look for the arguments' warrant statements and their simple claims and connect them to the proper claim and evidence statements. *Use connecting arrows* for this task. If warrant statements are implied, state them in the margin where the claims and evidence are presented.

4. Now that you have combined the claim, evidence, and warrant statements for each of the simple claims and the complex claims of the research piece, *place a box around each argument*.

5. Review the simple claim arguments. Are they correctly formed? If not, note the problem areas and revise them.

6. If the claims or arguments are incomplete, rewrite them.

First Draft: Evaluation

1. After completing the analysis, evaluate the arguments. Do they make the case? Begin by evaluating the major thesis statements.

   - Are the simple claims connected to a major thesis?
   - Are the simple claim arguments connected? Does the logic scheme of each argument work? Are the simple claims linked as cause-and-effect statements or perhaps as daisy chains?
   - Does the logic of the major argument make rational sense? If you find simple claim arguments that do not fit the logic scheme of the major claim, make adjustments.
   - If you find interesting fact statements that are irrelevant to the argument, remove them. Red herring statements and rabbit-run commentary present interesting information, but their inclusion into the argument scheme weakens the argument.

2. If you find the logical plan for the thesis argument lacking, revise it. Consider what warrant scheme can best link the simple claims into a pattern that will build the thesis arguments, then revise as necessary.

3. Does the research piece make its case?

First Draft: Outside Review

Taking drafts to an audience is central to each part of Task 2. For others to understand the writing, you must view the writing from an audience's perspective. Each person sees the world from a unique logic and vantage point. Others do not necessarily see your perspective. Because you are writing to be understood, you must transform the writing into language and logic that is effectively understandable to others. Once again, the outside review is crucial to this transformation. You must give serious thought to the plan for outside review before moving to the first and subsequent drafts. Here are a few points about selecting outside reviewers and drafting to be understood:

- Select outside reviewers for their expertise in the field. Choose some for their competence as writers and editors and others for their subject expertise. Ask each to review the work carefully and to give you a comprehensive response. The more specific and detailed the response, the better the revision. Remember, you are looking for a thoughtful, useful critique that adds value to the work.
- When preparing the draft for review, provide specific directions to the reviewer. Highlight areas that may need work. Have all reviewers comment on the readability of the work. Triple-space the draft to provide enough commentary space. Use line numbers for easy reference. To avoid confusion, date and number each draft.
- Set up a timetable for the return of the draft. Make time to review the returned drafts carefully. Arrange a time to discuss the returned drafts with each reviewer.
- Complete the auditing with all reviewers before moving to the second draft, third drafts, and any additional drafts. Integrate the revisions suggested by the reviewers. Clear up any conflicts between reviewers to your own satisfaction, then edit.

Activity 2. Revise—Working With the Second and Third Drafts

The edited first draft begins the transformation of your research into a work that is understandable to an outside audience. The purpose of the second, third, and any subsequent drafts is to refine the clarity and precision of the text so the work becomes the best rendition you can produce. Most changes made to the work now derive from specific audience response. Though you are writing for a large audience, recognize that the real audience is the specific person or group that will vet the work. This audience is either the instructor who will grade the effort or the committee that reviews the work. Those who vet the work should provide the advice necessary to polish the drafts and move them to the final published product. The goal of the second and succeeding drafts is to meet the expectations of those readers who are the arbiters and referees of the work. The key to the success of these later drafts is in the auditing you do to meet these expectations.

The guidelines used to conduct the audit of the first draft also work for polishing the later drafts. The audience changes for the refereed review. When auditing the second and succeeding drafts, have the instructor or committee review the work. Do this audit before the final submittal. If an instructor is grading the work, provide the polished draft for commentary. Provide plenty of time for the review. If a committee is responsible for approving the piece, work with the chairperson to develop a plan by which the committee can review the work and provide directions for suggested changes. Avoid surprises by refining the work to their specific expectations and specifications. Your task is simple: Make all suggested changes.

Activity 3. Completing the Final Draft

Writing the Final Draft

Polishing the final draft is a matter of refining the work to meet the expectations of those who will approve the publication. When considering later revisions, picture your audience. Think as they would think. Anticipate their standards for quality work. Revise your work from this vantage point. Remember to check once more that you have followed the writer's guideline or rubric if it is available for such a purpose. Review it carefully for suggestions and direction. Do a final check on the work's form and format by double-checking the approved style manual. Make revisions as needed.

Auditing the Final Draft

This is the last opportunity to make changes.

- Does the writing flow smoothly?
- Are all of the graphics, charts, and figures appropriately numbered and titled?
- Do a final check for proper form and format.
- Proofread, proofread, proofread.

TIPS ON WRITING

Good writing and an efficient process are essential for a successful literature review. Some tips for writing are as follows:

- Start with the main idea: Build its evidence, then summarize. After you have fully explored an idea, make sure there is a link (segue) to the next idea to bind the ideas and make a cohesive and coherent composition.
- In early drafts, write everything you know and want to say about the section of your topic. Do not stop to edit or rethink. Keep going.
- Initially, do not worry about grammar, spelling, or punctuation. Work at letting the ideas flow. The structure of the composition will be checked during auditing and editing.
- Use notes and outlines sparingly. Work at producing the writing from your head rather than from your references.
- Do not leave the notepad or keyboard until you have completed each section.
- Try not to end the writing session until you have charted the work for the next session.
- Be patient, be inquisitive, and be relentless. Do not leave the work until you have it exactly as you want it. Then expect to go back at it and rework it again.

LAST WORDS

If you follow the procedures discussed in this chapter, the writing of a literature review can be a rewarding experience. The key to writing a successful literature review is to be deliberative. Build a strong outline as the foundation of the work. Make sure the outline lays out the design of the composition and has enough details to give you a useful design for writing. Develop the composition in stages as two distinct tasks, first writing to understand and then writing to be understood.

Begin by writing an exploratory draft to transform the research to your perspective. Reconcile the exploratory draft to the research outline. This will build a strong foundation for the preliminary draft. Use auditing and editing to direct the revisions necessary for creating a quality first draft. Remember, use others to audit and provide advice to help mold the work into a composition that can be understood and accepted by the intended audience. Writing a literature review is not a complicated art form. Rather, it is an evolutionary sequence of writing and revising, with each revision shaping the composition until it tells the author's story with clarity and grace. The *act* of writing is not necessarily a joy; reading a well-written piece that you have worked through carefully is a joy. To have written is a joy as well. For that reason, *Carpe diem, quam minimum credula postero.* Seize the day, and put no trust in the morrow! Get on with the writing, and tenaciously follow it wherever it takes you. Craft it well. Experience the joy of completing a good work, of understanding and being understood.

> *Writing a book is an adventure. To begin with, it is a toy and an amusement; then it becomes a mistress, and then it becomes a master, and then a tyrant. The last phase is that just as you are about to be reconciled to your servitude, you kill the monster, and fling him out to the public.*
>
> —Winston Churchill (from a speech about his World War II memoirs delivered to Britain's National Book Exhibition, 1949)

Glossary

Argument: The presentation of one or more claims backed by credible evidence that supports a logical conclusion.

Argument of advocacy: An argument based on claims that have been proven as fact and that serves as the premise for logically driving a conclusion—in this case, the thesis statement of the literature review.

Argument of discovery: An argument proving that the findings of fact represent the current state of knowledge regarding the research topic.

Auditing: Reviewing completed work to check and align content and to proofread.

Backing: That which justifies the warrant.

Boolean search: A data search conducted using keywords connected by the logical operators *and, or,* and *not* to define the specific area of interest.

Claim: A declaration of proposed truth.

Complex argument: Arguments consisting of multiple claims formed to build premises that lead to a major thesis.

Complex literature review: This review extends the work of the simple review to identify and define an unanswered question requiring new primary research.

Core ideas: Central ideas that provide meaning to the interest statement under study.

Data: Pieces of information.

Deductive argument: An argument in which the premises necessarily imply the conclusion.

Descriptive reasoning: A process that examines data in order to identify or explain a phenomenon. It follows an if/then pattern. The *then* part is true when the *if* part has been proven.

Evidence: A set of data presented as the grounds for substantiating a claim.

Fallacy: An argument that leads to an erroneous or misleading conclusion.

Implicative reasoning: Reasoning that logically interprets evidence, producing propositions that signal a specific conclusion. If A is true, then we can assert that B is also true.

Inductive argument: Reasoning that moves from particular instance(s) to a general conclusion. The premises do not cause the conclusion, but the preponderance of evidence makes the conclusion likely or probable.

Key terms: Those words or phrases that control and define meaning.

Literature critique: A detailed analysis that interprets the current understanding of the research topic and logically determines how this knowledge answers the research question.

Literature review: A written document that develops a case to establish a thesis. This case is based on a comprehensive understanding of the current knowledge of the topic. A literature review synthesizes current knowledge pertaining to the research question. This synthesis is the foundation that, through the use of logical argumentation, allows the researcher to build a convincing thesis case.

Literature search: Collecting, cataloging, and documenting data that will determine salient works and refine the topic.

Literature survey: Building the argument about the current knowledge of the research topic.

Major claim: A major claim is based on the premises warranted by a complex argument. These premises are based on simple claims and their simple arguments.

Mapping: A technique that organizes the results of skimming to put the topic story together, building core idea and author maps and cross-referencing them.

Memoranda: Informal writing that includes a record of current activities and reminders of necessary further activities. Memoranda contain directive, advisory, and informative matter.

Personal interest or concern: The subject or question that provokes the need to inquire. This should not be confused with a preliminary topic.

Preliminary topic: A research interest statement that has been defined, limited to one subject of study, and linked to an appropriate academic discipline, enabling access to the relevant literature.

Premise: A previous statement of factor assertion that serves as the basis for a further argument.

Qualifiers: Data that demand rebuttal or concession and refute or limit the claim.

Reasoning: To discover, formulate, and conclude by the use of a carefully conducted analysis.

Reflective oversight: A contemplative thought process that critically regulates, assesses, and corrects the personal knowledge, skills, and tasks used to conduct the literature review.

Research query: A personal interest or concern that has been refined by focus, limit, and perspective.

Scanning: An organized search of library and online catalogs, subject-area encyclopedias, periodicals, indexes, and abstracts. The scan's purpose is to identify works for possible inclusion in the study.

Skimming: A rapid perusal of possible works to identify important ideas and their specific contribution to the research study and to determine whether or not to use the work.

Simple argument: Argument composed of a simple claim, its evidence, and its warrant.

Simple literature review: A written document that critically reviews the relevant literature on a research topic, presenting a logical case that establishes a thesis that delineates what is currently known about the subject.

Thesis: A declarative sentence that expresses a conclusion based on a case developed using existing knowledge, sound evidence, and reasoned argument.

Topic: A research area refined by interest, an academic discipline, and an understanding of relevant keywords and core concepts.

Warrant: The reasoning used in an argument to allow the researcher and any reader to accept the evidence presented as reasonable proof that a claim is correct.

Writing to understand: Journals, memoranda, notes, outlines, and all other forms of writing that allow the researcher to internalize the data, evidence, and arguments to be used in the literature review.

Writing to be understood: The preliminary, first, and subsequent drafts of a work that give the reader a complete and convincing understanding of the researcher's thesis.

References and Further Reading

Booth, W. C, Colomb, G. G., & Williams, J. M. (1995). *The craft of research*. Chicago, IL: University of Chicago Press.

Churchill, W. (1949). *A speech about his World War II memoirs*. Delivered at Britain's National Book Exhibition, London.

Cooper, H. (1998). *Synthesizing research* (3rd ed., Vol. 2). Thousand Oaks, CA: Sage.

Ehninger, D., & Brockreide, W. (1960). *Decision by debate*. New York, NY: Dodd, Mead & Company.

Fisher, A. (2003). *The logic of real arguments*. Cambridge, UK: Cambridge University Press.

Fisher, A. (2004). *Critical thinking: An introduction*. Cambridge, UK: Cambridge University Press.

Grennan, W. (1997). *Informal logic: Issues and techniques*. Montreal & Kingston, Canada: McGill-Queen's University Press.

Hart, C. (2001a). *Doing a literature review: Releasing the social science research imagination*. London, UK: Sage.

Hart, C. (2001b). *Doing a literature search: A comprehensive guide to the social sciences*. Thousand Oaks, CA: Sage.

Kelley, D. (1998). *The art of reasoning* (3rd ed.). New York, NY: W. W. Norton.

Mann, Thomas (2015). *The Oxford guide to library research* (4th ed). Oxford, UK: Oxford University Press.

Strunk Jr., W., & White, E. B. (2000). *The elements of style* (4th ed.). New York, NY: Longman.

Toulmin, S. (1999). *The uses of argument*. Cambridge, UK: Cambridge University Press.

Toulmin, S., Rieke, R., & Janik, A. (1984). *An introduction to reasoning* (2nd ed.). New York, NY: MacMillan.

Trimmer, J. F. (2004). *The new writing with a purpose* (14th ed.). Boston, MA: Houghton Mifflin.

Weston, A. (2000). *A rulebook for arguments* (3rd ed.). Indianapolis, IN: Hackett.

Williams, J. M. (1990). *Style: Toward clarity and grace*. Chicago, IL: University of Chicago Press.

Index

A SAGE Publishing Company

Helping educators make the greatest impact

CORWIN HAS ONE MISSION: to enhance education through intentional professional learning.

We build long-term relationships with our authors, educators, clients, and associations who partner with us to develop and continuously improve the best evidence-based practices that establish and support lifelong learning.

Solutions you want. Experts you trust. Results you need.